SELF HELPLESS

AND OTHER CONUNDRUMS

BY ERIC JAY SONNENSCHEIN

ISBN: 978-0-9861159-5-0

Cover design by Amanda Sonnenschein

TABLE OF CONTENTS

For Marilyn and Amanda

OPENING REMARKS

When I entered the adult world, I was stunned by how hard my life had suddenly become. I found myself in a constant state of confusion and dismay. All of the encouragement and praise I had received melted away and I was just another outstretched hand and hungry mouth, reaching and crying out for acceptance and approval. No one seemed to care about my potential or what I had done before. Naturally, I complained a lot about my situation.

Sooner than later, I realized that even if my problems were unique, facing difficulties was a typical debacle. It also became clear that whining was not making my issues go away and that if I didn't solve them, my life could be a mess until the very end. No one else was helping me, so I started to help myself. I considered how to improve my life in every way that it needed to be better. I had a lot of work to do.

Self-help offers strategies, not solutions. It cannot illuminate the unknown or bend the laws of chance but it is the only leverage I have against the power of fate.

At this point, I must raise an obvious question: what qualifies me to write self-help? I'm an expert in nothing but my own struggle. Yet this limited proficiency may be my strongest credential.

"Expert" advice often leaves us more confused than we were before, since two experts rarely agree. Ultimately, we must fall back on our own judgment, which we initially mistrusted, over which guidance to follow.

We learn best by perceiving patterns in the apparent disorder in our lives, not by heeding experts who see us from a distance and know only what we tell them.

I set out to write about what mattered most to me, objectives I'd pursued, troubles I'd seen and discoveries that added value to my life. If some passages in this book seem distorted and absurd, humor was not my primary motive for including them. Laughter is a fringe benefit, not the main event, but life, like many dramas, provides comic relief.

SWIMMING WITH A BRICK

I always had good health but never well-being, and it took me a while to distinguish between the two. Well-being begins with a wholesome routine that adds structure to one's life. A workout, a diet, an artistic discipline or a spiritual practice can all lift one above one's stressors and make problems seem insignificant. Most everyday phenomena we face can make us feel small and powerless, but simple self-therapies like regular exercise affirm our strength and provide stability and confidence.

The only caveat about a good routine is that it can make you smug and complacent. You may mistake the serenity and control you experience for invincibility, and believe that wholesome activity can extend your life and ward off aging. It is a psychological irony that even empowering regimens become ruts, desensitizing us while they boost endorphins. They become comfortable, rather than challenging, and lull us as easily as a couch.

My particular self-therapy is swimming. I swim laps as often as I can each week to stay fit, maintain flexibility and clear my head. A long swim also improves my mood and attitude. After a workout, I feel attuned to everything and disturbed by nothing.

I come alive in the water, regardless of how dead I feel when I go in, so the blasé attitude of most lifeguards baffles me. They sit poolside, often looking bored and miserable, and rarely enter the water. Is this what happens to anyone who converts a pastime into an occupation?

Yet, one lifeguard I know has never lost her love of the water. She comes early to her shift to swim laps and gets wet with her students when she's teaching them. Her love of aquatics is infectious. In her last adult beginners class, her students raced the length of the pool and dove off the board. For adult beginners, this qualifies as a miracle.

One afternoon, during a quiet moment in the pool, the water-loving lifeguard was swimming on her back in the next lane, with a black brick on her chest. She explained later that it was a lifesaving drill. I had never seen a lifeguard hone her craft in this way and her industry intrigued me.

Days later, I saw the same black brick on the bottom of the deep end. Normally I swim underwater, so when I notice objects on the bottom, like goggles or disks, I salvage them. It may be my way of "giving back," or a personal tribute to trained dolphins and pearl divers.

The black brick was an irresistible, even mythic lure to me. I imagined it as an amulet or a sunken treasure, and felt compelled to bring it to the surface and drop it on the deck. Near the end of my workout, I dove, grabbed the brick and lifted it. I had no idea how heavy it was.

My first test was to make it to the surface with the metal brick in one hand. I relied on a strong survival instinct to help me swim up through ten feet of water but once I broke the surface, how would I swim while holding the extra weight?

Doing a frog kick on my back with a brick on my chest is not part of my workout, so I resorted to a one-armed freestyle. Holding the brick in one hand, I stroked with my free arm. The 20 lb. brick made even floating difficult. I thrashed and splashed like a desperate novice to keep my head above water and to move with a modicum of speed in a general direction.

When I made it to the other end, I could not lift the brick and place it on the deck without standing, which would have broken my routine. So I left the weight in shallow water for future reference and finished my workout. After swimming one lap with a brick, I gasped for air for the next four. I was as tired as I had been when I started swimming years before.

After my workout, I handed the brick to the lifeguard.

"Thanks, I would have had to get it out before they vacuumed the pool," she said. My heroic exertion turned out to be nothing more to her than a perfunctory chore. But she had good news, as well. She confided that swimming while holding a person was easier than swimming with a brick because people are buoyant.

For days I lived with the after-effects of swimming with a brick—a back spasm, fatigue—and a more enduring and disturbing insight. Good actions can breed a false sense of security. I had believed that exercise made me strong and fit and prepared me for anything, yet just one added burden or unforeseen difficulty showed me how vulnerable I am.

BUTTERFLY UNDER GLASS

One benefit of being young, if you choose to see it this way, is that people are generous with their advice. The downside is that we can't often understand or use it until it is too late.

When I was new in New York, the people I stayed with introduced me one evening to their favorite hangout, a typical downtown bar with a jukebox and a pool table. A woman we met there, who was older than the rest of us, took an interest in my unsettled situation and stared at me significantly.

"You're a butterfly under a glass," the mantic woman said as she drew a sketch of this concept on a cocktail napkin and pushed it toward me. I thanked her for her art and her attention but her portent made me shudder with anxiety. Her metaphor was not strange to me, but eerily familiar. A variation of it had been applied to me only five years earlier.

In college I modeled for an oil painting. The artist depicted me as a pallid and elongated figure between two thick black columns. I seemed eternally trapped and pinned, with my eyes closed, as if interred.

The painting had an intriguing, if macabre effect at the time but I brushed it off as an artist's gimmick. However, this latest impromptu variation of a butterfly under an inverted glass struck me with fear. Was there something about me that evoked cruel captivity?

Only much later, when that evening at the start of my adult life was buried like a dead leaf under a decade of autumns, did the prescient woman's insight return to me as a clarifying caption of my life experience—and I finally understood what she meant.

An individual's freedom to plan a destiny and establish his identity, to be the person he wishes to become, is subject to and limited by the judgment and actions of other people.

Others put us in small boxes and we spend so much time and effort seeking the way out that we may realize too late that our struggle was

4

fruitless and unnecessary; that the only path to freedom is the one we find in ourselves.

I've seen this in my own life, but before I could see it, I had to feel it repeatedly, like lashes of self-flagellation on my back, because I blamed myself for not succeeding and believed I had to be doing the wrong thing.

When I was in school, I received much praise and encouragement for my writing, which confirmed my aspiration to be a writer.

However, when I set forth in the adult world I found no clear path to becoming a professional writer and the encouragements I had often received in the past were mocking echoes in the present.

I came to New York when I was 22 and the best job I could get, after a short stint in an army-navy surplus store, was selling advertising space for a weekly newspaper.

I wanted in the worst way to be a writer, but the managing editor, a veteran of local papers, refused to give me an assignment. He said an ad salesman was supposed to make money, not write articles. He made what he considered an irrefutable argument about the separation between the business and editorial functions of a publication.

According to this punctilious newsman, even my innocuous crossover between the commercial and editorial parts of the paper would do irreparable harm to its integrity and reputation. I pleaded with the managing editor that if he let me write for the paper, I would never tell a soul that I sold advertising space. I swore that I wasn't making much money at it anyway—although more than the $5 the publication paid for an article. To these entreaties he shook his head sadly and said there was nothing he could do—it was a line he couldn't cross.

It is impossible and of dubious value to speculate how this arbitrary prohibition changed the trajectory of my life and career. The managing editor didn't stop me from writing, but by barring this first step at a pivotal time of my life, he made it harder for me to turn my vocation into an occupation. Yet the psychological impact was worse. My sense that I was being held back in accordance with Procrustean norms filled me with frustration, resentment and an almost metaphysical grievance.

Except for being born into poverty, I'd always been favored by fortune—teachers and peers had often appreciated and encouraged me. But in New York, at this weekly newspaper, I believed life and the world had turned against me. My ambition was an endangered species.

This early setback taught me that all exclusions are traumatic, and the ones that seem less personal and most principled hurt the most. The cliché "It's not personal" exacerbates the pain because it suggests that there is no recourse or redress for your injury—it's "the way it is" and you must bear it stoically and without remedy.

"It's not personal" also belies one's logic and experience.

When the managing editor claimed I couldn't write for his fledgling low-circulation publication since I was traipsing all over the city trying to sell ad space for it, a fool's errand if there ever was one, he thought he had absolved himself for thwarting a young writer. He also believed he had softened the blow since he had not rejected me on merit but on principle.

To the contrary, his exclusion was more devastating because it precluded my challenge or appeal. I also saw through his excuse. Rules don't hold us back, people do. Rules only give them cover. The managing editor not only impeded my progress at this publication, but worse, he insulted my intelligence.

I found myself alone with my youthful aspiration. The only opportunities I had to earn a living, launch a career, or simply survive were jobs I didn't want.

Interviewers routinely chided me, "What do you want to do when you grow up?" as if my wish to be a writer was a childish preoccupation that I would—should—outgrow.

Yet I knew that the "big breaks" they offered would only break me; the "grown-up" careers would make my life miserable. Accepting second best would be like wearing the wrong colors, someone else's clothes or shoes two sizes too small.

As time passed, I grew increasingly frustrated and confused. There seemed to be a conspiracy of indifference toward my dreams. I was in a box and my only way out of it was to eschew the society of others, to renounce the idea of "fitting in," "knowing my place" and "accepting my fate" in a society of well-adjusted, mature people who accepted the roles accessible to them.

The demands my aspirations made on me were not aggressive but firm. I needed time and freedom, so I abandoned moneymaking ambitions, material comforts and a social life. I accepted these costs to save myself, but always felt acutely that I was missing out. Like anyone, I craved the company and affirmation of others, and expressing myself creatively was an indirect way to fulfill these needs. Yet ironically, I renounced such feedback for the freedom to express myself at all.

It was also clear that the society of others was a worthless burden to me if others could not see me as I wished to see and present myself. To play a character I didn't wish to play was to be an imposter, which was unacceptable. Meanwhile, to continue to be myself, without the approval and certification of the world, was to be strange, amorphous, and undefined in the eyes of others—a tangible kind of nothing.

When I was 21, my mother warned me about the necessity of "playing the game." She warned that I had everything to lose by refusing to do so. She urged me to join the military or work in a bank. I thought she was "low-balling" me, selling me so short on my potential that I could easily reject the compromise she proposed—which was probably not her objective. The prospect of failing, to my mind, could not be worse than a safe but distasteful alternative. I defiantly set out on my own.

But defiance is only a sprint that leaves one breathless and lost in the middle of nowhere, wondering where to go. If I clung to that state of mind, I would end up with no victory, only a stalemate, and my life would be thwarted.

I realized that the freedom and consciousness to define myself, regardless of what others had done, belonged solely to me. Others could slow me down, increase the distance I had to travel, frustrate and torment me with added labors and innumerable delays, and deny the legitimacy of my endeavors. They could wear me out and discourage me—*but I was the only one who could stop me.*

Although I dismissed, forgot and repressed the images of the thin, white man between thick black walls and the butterfly under the glass, these artistic renderings of my existence as someone held in and held back must have sunk to the bottom of my psyche, like a black box containing a secret code that transmitted a message from my unconscious that read, "You are stuck, doomed to fail, to be unfulfilled: get used to it or be consumed to death by it."

Maybe the gaunt man between the thick, black walls and the butterfly under the glass were two versions of a spell I was under. But then I broke the spell. My scrawny corpse broke through the thick, black walls. The butterfly fluttered, tapped and rapped against the glass with papery wings, and the glass tipped over and smashed.

It didn't end like a fairy tale. I didn't get the gold and live happily ever after. But I was able to find value in the life I was given and the one I made out of my choices and others' judgments. I was also able to experience the joy of living as the person I became rather than the person I wished to be.

The butterfly was my freedom and the glass was the judgment of others. It turned out that the black walls of the painting and the glass of the woman's sketch were not impermeable. But my fragile butterfly would never be entirely free.

There are times, on an otherwise relaxed Saturday morning, when I am off-guard, in my car, listening to an anodyne program on public radio, when a feature or interview is aired with someone whose talents have been discovered and applauded, whose vocation has become his job. He has submitted to the judgment of others and his self-belief has been vindicated and approved.

Suddenly, I revert to the butterfly in the glass and the emaciated cadaver between dense black walls. I am struck down and disconsolate. All

I can do to try to save myself from this eternal trap is to turn off the radio and surrender to speculation and self-pity. I wonder compulsively and redundantly what it might have been like to break through the dense black walls, to shatter that glass, to shine and be smiled upon, to be critically acclaimed by those respected for their opinion, to be validated and confirmed for life and posterity, to look in the mirror each morning and be able to say, "You are the person you wanted to be, doing what you aimed to do—and you are loved for it!"

These bleak moments also pass. I write and tune out others' judgments. I know I am so far from their awareness that their judgment cannot touch me. I may never receive their affirmation, but I can love myself. This is the only path to freedom I have—and most times, it takes me where I have to go.

FROM PRECOCIOUS TO LEFT BEHIND

When I was in primary school I basked in precocity. I loved to say wise things no one expected and watch the look of astonished delight on adult faces. I took pleasure in writing little essays and having the teachers return them with little "Wows!" in the margins and the longer notes, such as "This is astonishing. You know so much for someone so young." I loved getting good grades and hearing teachers praise me to my mother. In those days, being precocious was a ticket to wondrous places in the future. It meant having hope, and hope was the best friend I had.

Most people like gifted children if they are not obnoxious about it. In their bright faces and intuitive eyes, hard-bitten adults can relive vicariously their once unfettered potential.

In my case, precociousness resulted in skipping a grade. In high school I suddenly became the youngest person in my class. My acuity was still present, but it meant less. After all, the distance between one year and the next shrinks as one careers toward adulthood. Being young in my peer group did not confer the prestige and intrigue of the advanced child. To the contrary, it revealed less poise and self-control. I had opportunities for which I was not ready—being with a girl, driving a car without the slightest idea how to operate it, and other minor personal calamities.

My precocity, which had worked so well in primary school classrooms, was exposed in my late teens as brashness and poor judgment when I tried things I should have known well enough to avoid. I drank too much in my first year of college and passed out in the men's room during a party where I would have been better off talking to professors and socializing with peers. Or I drove a car into a tree because I did not know how to steer or brake. Or I had sex with girls without thinking about how they would feel when they realized that I had no serious feelings for them.

I was no longer precocious but *naïve*. I graduated from college and believed that people would embrace my talents even before I proved them. When I woke up from this delusion and tried very hard, I came to another, more crushing realization—that even one's best efforts and proven abilities don't guarantee success. This harsh fact nearly destroyed me. For several years, I vacillated between grief and rage until I finally overcame my bitterness about the mysterious vagaries of life.

But by the time I righted myself and decided what I would do with the life I was given, my former peers were far ahead of me, well along in their careers and earning good money. They knew who they were and where they belonged. They might not have been who I wanted to be but they were somebodies, while I was an embryonic nobody trying to become somebody while toiling to survive.

I realized I had been written off, uninvited to the big party of success and establishment where my peers were honored guests. I was now in perpetual remediation—writing by night and on weekends, holding day jobs all week that made me refractory and miserable. As I got older, I continued to nurse the potential that made me charming as a six year old but which now seemed superannuated and ridiculous.

Even poor circumstances become habitual. I adapted to solitude, to being an outsider, without friends or social life. Once I became accustomed to my diminished status, solitude closed around me like a skin.

Finally, strangely, I derived an unforeseen benefit from my slow progress, quiet life and social exclusion—I became a preternatural curiosity. When people don't hear from you for a while, they may assume you're dead. By being written off, I received a second life.

When I surfaced in the corporate job world because I had a family and needed a steady income, people who interviewed and hired me, and those I worked with, mistook my maturity and low job status as a sign that I was regressive, defective or unlucky. In the world's eyes I had gone from *can't miss* to a sad old misfit. Yet perhaps because they viewed me as such, I seemed no threat to them and they were willing to let an old dog do new tricks to assist and amuse them. They gave me a chance.

While people's views toward me had changed since my promising youth, I knew I was essentially the same person; I had not lost the gifts I had before—they were just no longer recognized or valued. That's when I realized what it meant to be underestimated.

At first I felt humiliated when people talked down to me. I grinned at them ironically when they explained their procedures slowly and asked me repeatedly if I had questions. My pride was hurt when they indulged and dismissed my statements because I wasn't supposed to say anything worthwhile.

Gradually I recognized that my mistaken identity as an old fool could be to my advantage. The real me was invisible. I surprised people when I opened my mouth and something other than drool came out. I worked harder, longer and better than anyone assumed I would. When people pushed me, I rose to their challenge and surpassed their expectations. Their bemused response to my unanticipated value was deeply gratifying.

It ought to have been easy to make up ground from left behind to back in stride. I expected my status to change as people realized who I really was. As I towered over their low expectations, I would be like the prince in rags who is discovered and restored to his throne, or like Marco Polo appearing in Venice after 25 years with firecrackers and a box of noodles.

I never considered that people would be irritated by my turnabout or that my lack of backwardness would disappoint anyone. By being smarter than they thought I was, I believed I became more worthy of my hire. But they preferred me as a mascot, a "project," a charity case. Beholding my true self made them acknowledge the painful fact that they'd made a mistake, which might throw their other calculations and criteria into doubt and disarray. Rather than be surprised and happy by an amazing and belated find of human talent they could rehabilitate and utilize, they viewed me as a fraud.

As I played with their heads, they played with their own. They were masters of their perceptions and could see me in whichever way they wished. They adjusted to my newfound ability by pretending it didn't exist, and reverted to their earlier manner of treating me. They ignored my comments and contributions, discounted my judgment and wasted my talents by assigning me mindless work to reinforce their expectations.

I cried out from behind the glass wall of their hostile indifference, "Hey, look and listen! I'm not who you think I am!" But they refused to hear me. They believed I had gained access to their privileged world under the false pretenses of my undervalued self. They mistook me for someone else and would never forgive me for it.

At that point, I realized that underestimation is a silence imposed by others—when you speak they turn off the sound in their heads.

Yet underestimation has advantages. When others are not listening, you can say what you want—repeatedly, if you wish, honing your rhetoric and message. If you stay patient, you may become stronger behind the barriers erected to exclude you as you wait for a door to open. When it does, you will cross the threshold nonchalantly like you always belonged inside. Some will doubtless consider you a trespasser, while others may appraise your contribution and acknowledge its value. This is the story I tell myself, at any rate, and thus far it has kept me going.

FEAT OF SELF-BELIEF

A prevalent theme of popular entertainments is the need to believe in others and in oneself. Yet in a time rife with fraud and flummery, and bereft of opportunities, belief in anyone or anything is more daunting than one would assume. Self-belief sounds as easy and basic as breathing and eating, but it requires enormous optimism, courage and will—almost to the brink of delusion. Many of our experiences tend to make us doubt ourselves, regardless of how ardently we struggle for confidence.

An acting teacher I know helps his students overcome "the problem of belief." To give an honest and compelling performance that seems real for the audience, the actor must make it real for himself, by believing the lines he speaks and the gestures and movements he makes. Without such belief, his performance will be flat or implausible.

For an actor, belief is a leap of imagination or an artistic problem, but for an individual in the world, belief is a necessity and losing it is a crisis. An actor need only believe he is someone else for a moment—if he falls short, he can try again, but an average person must believe what he does and says as himself. If his belief fails him, he may lose everything—his vocation, reputation, identity—even his character and soul.

By the time I was in my late 20s, I had not failed spectacularly or catastrophically, yet I was conscious of having started poorly. I convinced myself I must have missed a vital lesson in my education. Clearly, I had made missteps or lost traction.

On long, solitary evening walks I took stock of all I had done and failed to do.

For many years, I felt I existed outside the world, that I was doomed to an ordinary, interstitial existence, belonging to nothing and destined for nowhere. I had disappointed many people, most notably myself, by diverging from a well-worn path without finding and clearing my own.

I could not follow anyone, conform to anything or work my way up an organization ladder in a conventional manner. Nor could I persuade others to join me on my novel path. All of this was factual and clear. Yet despite my retrospective self-reproach, I could not determine when I let my chances slip away, or failed to seize my moment. The causes of my middling results remained mysterious. Finally, I settled on a provisional answer: I had done nothing wrong but I also hadn't done enough right.

I was like a racehorse that stumbled out of the gate. He might finish the race respectably but he'd never win. I had not been incarcerated; my record was clean. Yet, in terms of what I set out to achieve, I seemed to be serving a life sentence, as a captive of aspirations I would never reach.

At this rate, it was doubtful I'd come to be the person I wanted to be. I felt doomed to fall short. Yet I kept hope alive, locked up and hidden in a safe house in my heart. I reassured myself that that my prospects would unforeseeably improve. But as years passed, my circumstances hardened and my fate became transparent.

How many mornings in 20 years did I awaken with the persistent suspicion that I was wasting my life? When I was in my 20s and early 30s these primal concerns always led to a crossroads. An alternative route sprang up before me, as if by spiritual angiogenesis: I could get a profession or trade, attend law school, or earn a Ph.D. and teach. I mollified my doubts with hypothetical options I was unlikely to take.

However, these fallback plans did not bolster my self-belief. Like any palliative, the default option to abandon my vocation and flee my destiny did not breed confidence but eroded it. My self-doubt remained, a dense and amorphous cloud. It was frightening and destructive; I could not build a life on it.

Now that I've passed the threshold where potential gives way to inevitability, atavistic self-doubts no longer come with a bullet to bite, an off-ramp or an exit. A supervisor once aptly said that as we get older, doors close. Or to invert the idiom: opportunity no longer knocks.

Most doors are padlocked to me now. This is probably for my own good. I often refer to my choices in the past tense, as mistakes made and opportunities missed. Self-doubt is no longer a guest but a family member. I live with it because I cannot expunge it. My self-belief has been abraded by experience.

For much of my life, I wondered if I was deluded to pursue my goals. I wondered what I would do at the end of the cul-de-sac I was approaching. What would the awful reckoning be?

Histrionic? Perhaps. I struggled to live with my choices long after making them and to tolerate my mistakes. They are my eternal cellmates. I wonder each day if they were conscious errors or expressions of an inarticulate will so ingrained that I could not understand or change it if I wanted to.

In a material world of markets and competition, self-belief is precarious when it is self-generated, unplugged from public approval. Confidence flows more readily from the affirmation of others. How can I believe what I do is good if no one likes it? Work is supposed to earn rewards—money, popularity, fame or appreciation. We are what others say we are.

I experienced a total loss of confidence in my mid-twenties that persisted for years. I never sought treatment for it. Why would I bother? The cause was easy to deduce. I had succeeded in youth, but in "the real world" had experienced nothing but rejection for all my creative undertakings. I was sick, frustrated and lonely—unable to fulfill my needs, feed myself or make friends.

Even my safety and survival were in doubt. I found myself surrounded by enemies on the street who would threaten me with baseball bats and other primitive and effective weapons from the Bronze Age.

I had failed in every pursuit and my failures had brought me no closer to illumination or material success.

In this famine of affirmation, I lost confidence in my judgment and doubted my ability. I no longer trusted myself to make good decisions. Only now years later do I realize how little self-belief I had.

For the first time in my life I acknowledged I had no idea what was going on around me, what people thought, or how to connect with them. I ascribed my lack of success to my obtuseness and not to the competitive environment and the difficulty of my pursuits. I was paralyzed by confusion and self-doubt.

Then I met my future wife. She had the equable temperament I lacked and a clear vision of how the world worked and what people thought and felt. I consulted with her frequently—about everything. She tutored me on what to do and say with others and how to respond to what they did and said—so that I might survive as an adult among strangers.

As with a language course, I reviewed with my tutor what I had done or said each day. We evaluated my performance and determined where improvements could be made. I avidly applied myself to her tutelage since my lack of success convinced me that I had been wrong about everything.

Self-belief regenerated slowly. It did not follow the seasons but its own inscrutable process of renewal. Though guided by a gifted and dedicated teacher, I went through the motions of my new life with no intuitive grasp of what I was doing. As I waited for a new perspective to develop, I translated the new world through my old eyes. As my confidence took root, I acted as if I already believed in myself.

It is unclear in retrospect when, how and why my recovery occurred. There was no turnaround in my fortunes. It is possible that through trial and error I grew familiar enough with people and situations to deal with them effectively and with less ambivalence. Or I concluded that since I had already ruined my life, I could do no worse. I relaxed and acted instinctively, having noted that what I did or said at a given moment played only a small part in any outcome. I ceased to look for reasons to blame and castigate myself for the past, and stopped obsessively probing for the pivotal blunder I thought I must have made to ruin everything.

Eventually my confidence returned. Years passed. I changed. The nature of self-belief was also transfigured, with a new ambit and meaning.

What doubts I had about my ability faded when I no longer measured it by outcomes. I arrived at a new understanding: confidence sprang not from my insights, attributes or achievements, but from my will to survive.

I no longer expected to understand the world, or even *my* world. I no longer believed I controlled my destiny, or that everything in my life resulted from what I did, said, or decided. My life wasn't even all about me.

When our daughter was born, I had to provide. The two people I loved most on this Earth depended on my resourcefulness. I needed faith not only in myself but in others. Would they who had given me the back of their collective hand, now give me a chance to raise my family?

The odds against my success were long. My relationship with others had always been fractious. I fit in society like an unwanted orphan and I resented it. But without the legitimation of others, my self-belief was worthless; I would be pounded slowly into dust.

My self-belief resurged out of necessity. My family depended on me so I couldn't fail. What would happen to them if I did? I had to be confident so they would feel safe with me. For several years I was able through ingenuity and luck to earn enough money to pay for living expenses and our daughter's nursery school. My confidence grew but it was not truly tested until I came to a daunting obstacle—my teaching contract would not be renewed, so I had to find a new occupation and a full-time job.

Confidence, like any other quality, must be tested in order to be strong. One must face a crisis, endure a tribulation or take a difficult stand to give it permanence. Middle-aged and changing careers, I looked for months for a job without success. Yet I did not falter or flinch. I knew our situation was dire but I never felt it or betrayed it to my wife and daughter. I knew what it was like to grow up in an insecure household with pernicious money problems and I never wanted my child to bear this emotional trauma.

I finally overcame the ordeal. Finding a job in a new career under pressure was an enormous relief—the world and I seemed finally aligned. However, my confidence was forged not by traversing the abyss but by facing it with calm fortitude. After staring down the prospect of raising a family on no income, I could always tell myself, "If you got through that you can get through anything." Confidence doesn't come with a certificate but if it did, those words would be the motto inscribed on it.

Emerging from this tight, dark corner, I became aware of myself in a new way. I had felt enormous stress but no despair, and I possessed a quality I undervalued—tenacity. Everything in my life past and present became clear. Self-belief flowed back as I understood the most important attributes I had: I was stronger and more resilient than I had known.

Being a parent increased my confidence. I saw my child go through vicissitudes that I could recall going through myself. I could not experience her emotions or relive my life in hers, but as I guided and reassured her, her learnings became my reflections. As I watched her grow up I realized that I had not imagined or exaggerated the challenges of my young life I still vividly remembered.

My self-belief was restored to me by a series of subtractions. I had lost confidence by clinging to aspirations and believing in abstractions. But when I perceived the true shape and substance of my life and accepted its gifts and strictures; when I renounced permanence and accepted impermanence; when I relinquished perfection and relished the excellent and the good; and when I accepted that most of what I did was due to trial and error—mainly error—my self-belief was restored.

The quicksand of living is the bedrock of faith. The feat of self-belief is not contingent on results. It requires that one believe in everything and nothing, and cope with ignorance and uncertainty. In the slow accretion of experience, it is clear that nothing is knowable. Reading people and circumstances, like predicting outcomes, is only guesswork.

Self-belief is not about believing in yourself alone but in a power that carries you from error to wisdom and from agony to peace, which are the only gifts you may get from life if it gives you anything at all and you're ready to receive them.

THE ART OF LIVING AND THE ART OF STAYING ALIVE

A Personal Art Form and Salvation

The art of living is the only art that purely benefits the artist. Rather than put him on a limb, it centers him. It does not deplete his health and undermine his sanity but fortifies him in the struggle to survive.

This noble craft requires insight, study, practice and skill, yet it can also be viewed as a selfish and exclusive art form, since it is only on exhibit for those who know the artist best. Its galleries are where he goes. Its master works are his serenity and satisfaction, the well-being he exudes and his self-actualized smile.

The art of living also confers a benefit on anyone with whom the artist interacts, yet its principal achievements are privately collected, not for public consumption. Because its practice is quotidian, idiosyncratic, and its media diffuse, the art of living is rarely acknowledged or discussed. There is no agreement on its aesthetic because few people know it exists.

We are often content to live in careless spontaneity or unconscious habit, without the forethought or embellishment that transform raw matter into finished art, time into time well spent. We do what a moment requires without reflecting on how to improve it, and without noting what we did well so we can replicate it.

The art of living is as subjective as any other art form but for me it is predicated on a simple truth: my life is important to me, and every action I take and every gesture I make has meaning and effect—not symbolic and hypothetical, but tangible and real.

Religions may aim at similar goals, but with the art of living my activities are significant, not because they affect the cosmos or my status with respect to a deity, a creed, an afterlife, or an infinite life continuum, but insofar as they embellish or detract from my temporal existence here, now, today and tomorrow.

Time cannot be extended, yet we can fill each second to the brim. Anyone who appreciates the value in repeating a thing done well and who wishes to make the most of every moment, regardless of when, where or in what degree of comfort it is spent, perceives the art of living as a personal salvation. It filters randomness from our lives and replaces accident with intention. It gives us the power to build something from ourselves and for ourselves that is substantial and grand out of the odds and ends circumstance foists on us.

The unheralded virtuosity of creating a good life out of a myriad of deft choices will absorb much of our energy and attention if we are mindful in its undertaking. We will acquire and employ the finer things we wish for ourselves. We will always strive to look, feel and do our best, find the right clothes to wear and make our homes pleasant to live in. The art of living is an egocentric art but not an egotistical one. We practice it modestly without expecting it to be acknowledged or perceived.

This is no frivolous pursuit or art for its own sake. It extends beyond itself to produce a radiant benefit: the satisfaction an individual derives from a life well lived affects those around him as well as his environment.

The art of living does not depend on ideal conditions, a complete palette or a sophisticated palate; it requires only that we use what we have to the optimal effect. Yet, this most practical and elusive skill presupposes that you have enough of what you need. It does not call for a perfect moment but a peaceful and stable environment that complies with your desires and permits you to create.

The Art of Staying Alive

To ply the art of living, the artist controls his tools and his medium. However, control is a cultivated skill, not an inherent virtue—aspirational, not fundamental. The art of living can be subverted by stress, as the artist's will encounters obstacles malignly planted to thwart him.

Since we often lack control over basic aspects of our lives, we must adapt the art of living to circumstances that are fluid, uncertain and even inimical to our desires. The ensuing variation is a dark art form in which our choices are not entirely our own but are negotiated. This is the art of staying alive.

If the art of living is based on having, the art of staying alive is predicated on never having enough, of being obliged not merely to "make do" but to make something out of nothing. The art of living can stretch our ingenuity and imagination, but the art of staying alive tests our mettle and resolve. The art of living may force us to adjust, while the art of staying alive forces us to endure pain—because there is always pain in survival.

Brazilians have a term, *jeito*, to express the dark art of staying alive. I discovered the word in a picture book about Rio de Janeiro, which I won as a telemarketer after selling six books over the phone. It was the perfect context for learning about this magical concept because *jeito* was what I lacked and needed most.

Jeito is all about getting from A to Z, when B through Y are in the way. It is a game of constant challenge that rewards ingenuity, cunning and finesse. It is a game I never liked to play because it seemed like a waste of creativity, but my life improved when I started to embrace this gritty, wily art form since it compelled me to solve problems on a regular basis. This annealed my mind and prevented a mental breakdown.

The guiding principle of *jeito* is that problems never end. Life is never easy, regardless of how well we adapt to it. Complications and exceptions are the norm and complacency is not an option we can afford to take. As soon as we become comfortable, someone or something comes along to disrupt our peace and send us scrambling for new coping mechanisms. The art of staying alive is an improvised dance of pratfalls and contortions.

As in most cities, parking a car on a New York street is impossible. Even in my somnolent upper Manhattan neighborhood, parking is absurdly difficult since real estate agents, in their nefarious zeal to attract business, lure apartment-seekers with the false promise that they can find easy parking for their vehicles here. Though they suffer these harsh facts collectively, today's residents maintain a conspiracy of silence about the local parking crisis because they want prospective buyers to believe the same false promise of easy parking and prop up the value of their property. In a sense, they're all collaborators in a real-estate marketing Ponzi scheme.

Since parking is a nightmare at all hours, it seems incredible that anyone could or would exacerbate the situation. Yet in the past year, a new charter school has appropriated a large number of spots from 7AM-4PM. They have turned the existing scarcity of spots into a parking famine. So how can one react? By expanding one's circle—seeking parking spots where one would not have looked before. During the day, one may leave one's car in the park for four hours or in the adjacent neighborhood, where street-sweeping days and hours differ from our own.

But for many residents in this neighborhood neither of these options is satisfactory. They have adapted to the parking rules by sitting vigil in their cars for 90 minutes once a week in the middle of the day, as they wait for the street to be cleaned. When the sweeper comes by, they move their cars to accommodate it, after which they immediately return to their precious spots and squat in them until the no parking period is over. Then these zealous parkers leave their vehicles in their coveted spaces until the next week, when they give an encore performance of the parking dance.

Rather than drive their cars normally and look for parking for 15, 20 or 30 minutes when they return, these determined parkers prefer to waste 90 minutes in one shot to secure a place by the curb. Meanwhile, they drive their vehicles only on rare occasions, suggesting that their driving machines are no longer *mobile,* but large stationary objects, like dumpsters.

These stubborn neighbors have devised a time-consuming strategy to obtain one advantage; yet by seeking convenience, they only redistribute inconvenience. They may believe they're being "street smart," "getting over" on life and "doing what they have to do" but in trying to save time and avoid an onerous regulation, they miss the core principle of the art of staying alive, which is to avoid traps, not fall into them.

This is the opposite of *jeito,* which does not convert one misfortune to another, but solves a problem so that life can be enjoyed again until the next problem appears. *Jeito* is a temporary victory over obstacles to happiness and convenience, yet those who stew in their cars for 90 minutes only to leave them in the same spot for a week do not triumph over anything. They park rather than drive, and pay exorbitant insurance and other car-related expenses without obtaining a commensurate benefit.

Contrast these hyper-vigilant parkers with a true grand master of *jeito*. He is a vocal atheist who scorns organized religion. He is also a card-carrying reverend in the Church of Everlasting Life, a denomination anyone can join. After he completed an easy form on their website and paid a nominal fee, the church sent him a card that certified his ministry.

"The Reverend" has used this card strategically during traffic stops. A local policeman sees the card and asks, "Are you really a minister?" "Yes, I was going to tend to a sick member of my flock," the Reverend explains. "All right, get out of here and slow down!" the cop replies. He is furious with himself for granting this religious exemption but he can't bring himself to challenge the first amendment protection of religious freedom.

That is pure *jeito*. It does not change or resist reality, but plays with it. It creates an interval of freedom and relief before the next crisis, indignity or inconvenience must be confronted. It is the art of getting by.

Staying Alive and Extending Life

One morning I received an unexpected phone call from my daughter. "Is everything okay?" I asked.

"I had a terrible dream," she replied. "I dreamed that you died. And I couldn't do anything. Mommy and I were printing out photographs. I felt so sad and helpless."

My daughter who rarely cries was now sobbing so hard that she had me crying, too. I felt terrible and I hadn't even done anything. I consoled her by explaining that it was normal for her to worry about my passing since I am much older than she is. I pointed out that the tragedy would be if I didn't die before she did. I also admitted that I once had a similar dream about her and my wife, and it was so awful that I suppressed it and wouldn't admit that I dreamed it.

"It's normal to worry about losing the people we love," I assured her. I told her that I was sick with concern when she moved out to Los Angeles after college, especially since she had never lived on her own and had not driven much either. "But I couldn't chain you to the bed to make sure you were safe. Loving and the fear of losing go together."

Gradually, I shifted the conversation to my upcoming birthday and her birthday three weeks later and I reminisced about all of the previous birthdays we had celebrated going back to when she was two years old—when she had her first party. She calmed down and my wife analyzed her dream as a displaced anxiety about her upcoming film shoot.

But such a moment doesn't fade. My daughter's dream struck me hard because recently I also had thoughts about dying soon. I don't know why I had them more now than before. Maybe I always had them but used to be better at suppressing them. Now I'm older and the possibility of death is closer and more probable. My morbid streak might have been triggered by strange looks people were giving me of late. I wondered if my daughter had been telepathically intercepting my morbid thoughts.

I reassured my distraught child that I was doing all I could to stay alive. I enumerated for her all the life-extending measures I was taking: I exercise every day, prepare wholesome foods, abstain from smoking tobacco and drinking alcoholic beverages. I drink homemade lemonade for vitamin C and avoid all foolish risks and unnecessary exertions.

This, I pleaded, was all anyone could do to stay alive. Yet, even as I laid out my plan for life extension, I acknowledged how absurd it was to confront death with these anodynes. It was like throwing spears at fighter jets.

Before I got off the phone, it occurred to me that my daughter and I were seeing death in the wrong way. Neither of us understood it or could do much about it. It was better to turn from the unknowable to what we knew with certainty—how important we were to one another and how great a part we had played in each other's lives.

"You can't keep someone alive if it is their time to die," I said, "but you can make them want to live. You've given me great joy from the moment you were born. This is all you can do. No human being can do more."

As our conversation assumed a calmer tone, I promised my daughter that I would do everything in my power to stay alive as long as possible. This made us both feel better, though I knew I was being grandiose and deceptive. We need to feel we have power over our lives but all we can do is live them.

The Art of Living in the Shadow of Death

Reassuring my daughter that I did all I could to stay alive was sincere but meaningless. After all, the art of staying alive is a knack for getting by, not prolonging life, which is out of one's hands. How could I put the odds of life in my favor when life and death are too powerful and pervasive to do anything but deride any numbers I might cite to predict their mysterious ways?

Even when mothers and doctors admonish us to take care of ourselves, to get our sleep and eat right, to take our vitamins and avoid undue stress and dangerous risks, they are not telling us how to prolong life, but only how to avoid risk factors for untimely death. That is all the art of staying alive can do—help one avoid hastening the inevitable.

For the entire day after hearing my daughter's portentous dream, I was under a nimbus of foreboding. I lived each moment as if I were on death row and scheduled for execution. I was at times short of breath and experienced suspicious pains in my arm, my chest and later in other body parts. Was my time at hand? Should I even swim or would this daily exercise finish me off?

At such times I realize how much I love life and why I practice the art of living and the dark art of staying alive. Despite my problems, real and perceived, at that moment I refused to accept my imminent demise. I talked myself down from the hypochondriacal ledge where I was perched with the sensible observation that if I were in mortal danger, as I believed I was, the receipt of a parking ticket or another minor stressor could also be the end of me.

Thus encouraged, I swam according to my routine. At first I took it slowly. But then without asking permission, my body took over and it worked with greater speed and resolve. I felt strong and alive again. It was hard to believe that I was the same person who had morbidly anticipated a sudden demise. Yet even as I enjoyed my vigorous swim, I wondered if my strength and well-being could be a "false positive," a halcyon oasis of good health, like a winter thaw before an Arctic vortex.

The Art of Living and the Bane of Illness

Sometimes the art of living devises strategies that oppose normal practices and precautions. The artist of living must defy his moods and physical discomforts. For instance, when I'm ill, conventional wisdom prescribes rest, fluids and patience until the pathogen clears. But rest can feel like capitulation, which exacerbates my malaise and physical symptoms. As I lie in bed, my body may rest but my soul languishes. Regardless of the health plan, my soul is my physician.

Recently, I had an ingenious flu-like virus, the kind that does not incapacitate its host but brings on fatigue, weakness and agitation. I might have spent each day in bed but I had second thoughts. It was dubious that lying in bed would make me physically better, but I knew it would make me psychologically worse.

So I persisted in my routine. I swam a kilometer as usual and took a shower. For several days the showers where I swim had lacked hot water. Most people avoided a workout if they couldn't top if off with a hot shower so I had the locker room and pool to myself. At first, my swimming was labored but the water soon embraced me and the steady, repetitive strokes kept me warm. Finally, halfway into my workout, I felt invigorated and strong. Where did this strength and well-being come from?

Even the cold shower did not faze me, since it had been part of my regimen for years. Cold showers started as a cheap summer alternative to air conditioning but I continued to take them to strengthen my will and increase my capacity to endure stress. Cold water is uncomfortable but you get used to it, and when you turn it off, the air feels warm. I also have read that cold showers increase circulation and boost the immune system.

For a month this walking flu plagued me, yet I didn't miss a day of swimming and cold showers. I dreaded my workout, but during and after it were the only times I felt healthy and in good spirits. This is where the arts of living and staying alive intersect.

Second Thoughts and Final Reflections

I've given much thought and effort to the art of living, yet my practice falls short in one respect—I haven't applied it to my interactions with others. Over time, as I focused on improving the quality of my life, I became less gregarious and stopped trying to persuade others to share my vision. It is unclear if this is a personal foible or intrinsic to the art, itself.

The art of living draws upon many sources, yet each of us develops it in a unique and personal way, befitting our respective tastes and aptitudes. Sharing this art form and its benefits would be ideal, but the individual perspective on which it is based may make collaboration difficult, if it is possible at all.

I wish to make my time on Earth more enjoyable and worthwhile. However, if I fail to work at staying alive, the art of living will be art for art's stake because hassles, illness and an obsession with death will blunt the finest small triumphs of ingenuity.

Life is often dreary but it's like a junkyard—joy is strewn among the abject and broken parts. The art of living forages for joy and finds it, while staying alive manages the amorphous, chaotic catastrophe in which life presents itself to us, so we have ample time and energy to delight in it.

Staying alive is a personal practice. The only useful instruction or guidance a stranger can provide about it is that it exists and ought to be learned on your own terms. To start, you must be honest with yourself and take stock of what you need and the challenges you face in obtaining it.

This is not as simple as it sounds. We overlook our true needs as much as we ignore our weaknesses and exaggerate our strengths. We live in reality, yet it is always difficult to face up to it: we need courage for that.

The arts of living and staying alive may not be fine arts but they are bold and ingenious ones. The artist works with bits and pieces to achieve an impermanent effect with no illusion of immortality or transcendent value. Even at their best, these arts are no more than improvisational means for provisional ends.

Life is never perfect. It often doesn't even rise to the level of good. So goodness and satisfaction must be our goals. With the paltry materials life provides, we may be unable to create a masterpiece, at least not within the standard parameters of the word. The range of life-arts is not the timeless and the pure, but the cyclical and the ordinary. The most we can aspire to is to create something each day, even for a moment, that pleases or inspires us.

BROTHER, CAN YOU SPARE ME SOME TIME?

Recently, I was driving home in heavy traffic. It was a 40-minute commute that would take an hour and a half. I listened to the radio with more than usual attention, hoping it would lift my spirits a few notches above my misery. I was rewarded with an unending stream of interviews, features, endorsements and ads for products and services that promised to reduce work, optimize time, save money or make more of it.

One radio personality touted a flashlight that moonlights as a pen and can break your windshield if you're stuck in your car while plunging into a raging river. Another pitchman promoted a workshop to bring me success, a self-image, and a sex life. A deluge of ads and reviews exhorted me to see films, read books, and visit amusement parks—all to enhance my time.

These products and proposals were clearly the clever residue of many brilliant minds—yet they sounded alike. Their creators seemed locked in a box. There was only one product I wanted while I was squeezed between two SUVs in a toll plaza; only one invention I would pay for. Wouldn't you know that it was the one item nobody thought to manufacture?

I needed something to make more time or to stretch the time I had. It could be a time supplement that came in a pill, a powder, herbs or a protein shake. With my time dwindling in traffic, I would pay $19.95 with shipping and handling for anything that would replenish my time.

"Brother, can you spare me some time?" I brayed at the radio, "If you don't figure out how to give me more of *that* I can't do, see, hear, eat, drink or earn enough money to pay for a fraction of what you're selling me."

Just the night before, I woke up in a sweat from a familiar dream. Maybe you have had one like it. Chased by killers, I ran, but my legs were leaden and my feet sank in clay that hardened around my ankles. I was stuck in a bog of concrete. The dream concluded when I said, "Relax, it's only a dream," and I shot up in bed. My eyes bulged and I gasped for air. I was sure I was dying but I wasn't going quietly. I dashed to the bathroom, splashed water on my face and attempted to return to normal. But there was no point in trying to fall back to sleep because I never woke up. I live this nightmare everyday.

I try efficiency and trust technology but I can't beat deadlines, avoid last-minute crises or complete my projects before my time runs out.

Seize the day? I can barely get my mind around it. Details compound hourly. The more I have to do, the less time I have, and the less I do with it. I drive here and stop there. I send this, buy that, phone this one or text that one, I scavenge for parking, eat, wash dishes and take out garbage. It's already late. I am wired and tired and there is less time to manage it all.

Time is the hardest substance to control. The more discipline I have, the more of this precious thing I squander. I can't prevent myself from thinking random thoughts, pondering the past, watching TV, listening to music, researching random facts and cooking from scratch—all time-consuming activities. I am an ostrich with his head in the sands of time.

I reassure myself that there is hope for the expansion of time. After all, for one day each year we come close to making time—the 25th hour on the first Sunday in November. But *Fall Back Sunday*, the return of Eastern Standard Time, is a bookkeeping trick, not our greatest invention. It is a loan of an hour paid back to us, interest-free.

Nonetheless, *Fall Back Sunday* suggests that we have our minds on the problem. We're working on the expansion of time, and for that one day, we see how miraculous that extra precious hour is, to sleep—or to dream. I have always treasured this lagniappe, even when I woke too early and waited for everyone else to catch up with me.

Now even this boon is being ravaged by hidden fees—the details of modern living. My last *Fall Back Sunday* I used the gift of time to adjust watches, clocks, TVs, radios and devices. When all was reset, the 25th hour was gone and I was back to wasting the usual 24.

Time is everyone's problem, so why should I seek anyone else's advice about how to manage it? Bookstore shelves are stocked with self-help titles that promise to save time if I will put in the time to read them. But I would need an afternoon to browse for the right book and spend another week absorbing the ingenious strategies—many of which I have tried, and none of which will save even a second after I factor in the time I need to incorporate them.

State of the art gadgets and devices presumably save time but I would have to read the instructions and understand how they work. Then I would need to spend hours on the technical support line when the devices failed to function as promised or I misunderstood the directions.

I am no Luddite railing against progress. I marvel at the sleek machines and respect the people who design them. I also envy and admire the management gurus who write best sellers on how to manage time. What magicians they are!

Back at the toll plaza, I eased and squeezed my way among trucks and buses as radio pitches, promotions and endorsements bombarded me with how to spend time and money in order to save money and time, so that I could spend the time I'd saved by spending more money. Pressure mounted, spasmodic traffic nauseated me and I struggled to breathe through a panic attack.

The bombast had exploded into a truth. I perceived the blindness of these wunderkinds and the pathetic folly of this age in which I was blessed to be alive. I felt suffocated by our lack of progress in the production of time and the incessant chatter that distracted us from our manic stagnation.

"I need more time!" I shouted at the radio before I turned it off and smacked the dashboard. The truth about time transfigured my face as I gesticulated. It enraged me that the moguls and mental giants on the airwaves could not add a second to my life. Yet, to be candid, the genius who might accomplish this feat existed only in the pantheon of my dreams. "Give me more time!" I cried out repeatedly to no one in particular.

This desperate outburst was taking place in the privacy of my car and I believed my doors and windows protected my speech from public judgment, yet the driver in the next lane and his four passengers gawked at me in alarm. I hoped they wouldn't call 9-1-1.

One day engineers will see that time saving is another guise for time wasting. They will not bother with a smaller computer, a more powerful chip or a more efficient operating system. They will devote themselves to a machine that makes time, like a snow-machine at a ski resort.

Meanwhile, artists will no longer devise new ways to kill time but to create it. According to Blake, energy is delight—true, *but time is life.* Picasso produced artworks to fill several museums but not one hour in which to view them. Even Da Vinci, the consummate artist-inventor, never applied his capacious imagination to the increase of time, nor sketched a machine to make more of this most precious substance. How much would a synthetic minute bring at Christie's? I would trade every timesaving device for one extra hour. But I will never find it for barter or sale.

How did I fall into a gap between the time I have and the time I need? I have 3 theories: political, historical and conspiratorial.

- Political: The American ethos is to blame. Frustrated by an egalitarian democracy, I try to lift myself above others by making the most of my time, while others do the same to me.

- Historical: Current time-devouring complications are the result of a service economy that does not manufacture goods but instead spews more rules and procedures.

- Conspiratorial: A multilateral government commission has devised every time-wasting complexity from mass-transit to banking to doctor appointments. Their objective is to devalue my time so I will die willingly at retirement age rather than extend life and draw social security.

When these conjectures do not form a coherent theory, I turn to a psychological explanation. My problem is not about time, space, or society, but only my expectations. I cannot attain the unattainable. I over-reach, under-sleep, devour with my eyes and stuff my face, plan more than several lifetimes can contain and forfeit the wisdom of years for the dilatory wishes of youth. Tantalus, pass the grapes.

NOSTALGIAS

I often reflect on the past when I try to solve a problem or settle my nerves in the present. The past is a convenient stop on an existential errand because it does not appear to move or change, and it is far enough away to see clearly.

Yet I have found that a mind wandering endlessly over the foggy landscape of the past is far from quiet or settled and it cannot be certain of what it perceives in scale or detail. History is a vast immutable expanse that resides in the seismic mind and does not decay so much as condense. Like a cloud, it covers, flows and slips between the hapless fingers of memory as we try to gather and reconstitute it.

Memory is mechanical and limited, a poor instrument for assembling truth. Yet its defects make it a useful projector of our dreams and fantasies—the ones we create from the lives we've lived, half-remembered, half-forgotten and entirely imagined.

Even if you deem yourself a pragmatic, positive individual, unsentimental and impervious to the past, you may be vulnerable to nostalgia. If only for that unguarded moment one morning when you wake up wishing you felt as good as you did before, had the energy you once had, or could move without twinging joints, you are susceptible to reveries of the good old days.

There are now 65 million "baby boomers" between 50 and 70 years of age. When 20% of a national population approaches or reaches retirement, nostalgia becomes a primary emotion that assumes epidemic proportions with unimaginable consequences.

The broadest definition of nostalgia is a longing for something in the past. However, since humans lack one fixed and universal nature, we need more than one of every attitude—including nostalgia, which comes in three varieties. Many of us experience each of these three forms of melancholy at one time or another. They are positive nostalgia, negative nostalgia, and *saudade,* a Portuguese/Brazilian form of free-floating nostalgia that incorporates the other two, but extends beyond them.

Positive nostalgia, which Shakespeare coined as "a remembrance of things past," is the strain of nostalgia we typically think of, since it is has often been expressed in music and film. Positive nostalgia is a wistful and misty-eyed harkening back to an experience of life as fresh and exciting. It typically involves childhood and teenage fun, young crushes and falling in love, adventures with friends and such threshold events as proms, weddings and graduations.

Implicit in positive nostalgia is the belief that life as a whole was better *then,* and that everything comprising it was also better *then,* including weather, traffic jams, and plumbing fixtures. People with a bad case of positive nostalgia may wish to bring back old supermarket chains, like Grand Union and A&P. They want women's padded shoulders to make a comeback. They wish the "Archies" would go on tour, although they never gave a live performance. These *nostalgiacs* want old cars with carburetors and spark plugs you can change on your own. They want cheap gas and vinyl LPs, hip-huggers and earth boots, bookstores and record stores to magically reappear. They want to be bullish with Merrill Lynch and to "make money the old-fashioned way by earning it."

Positive nostalgia is the reason we show up at reunions, tune into classic rock radio and flock to golden oldies revues. It permeates our culture. Don McLean's *American Pie,* Bryan Adams' *Summer of 1969,* Jackson Browne's *Running on Empty,* Frankie Valli's *Oh, What a Night* and Bowling for Soup's *1985* are some musical examples of positive nostalgia.

Films too have tapped a vein of longing for simpler, sweeter times. Francis Ford Coppola's *Peggy Sue Got Married,* George Lucas's *American Graffiti* and Federico Fellini's *Amarcord* are among many motion pictures that have comforted and beguiled us with a halcyon past. TV has also been a nostalgia-mill, producing a revival of the 1950s with *Happy Days* and *Laverne and Shirley* and more recently serving up blasts from our past like *That 70s Show, Mad Men* and the Australian serial *A Place to Call Home* in order to indulge our wish to go "back in the day."

The tonic message of positive nostalgia is that life was better when we were younger, but implicitly we know that this is only half of the story. A significant part of us, the ironic, mature part, concedes that the innocence, awkwardness and uncertainty of youth were not entirely wonderful, that to the contrary, they carried a freight of humiliation and pain. Since we believe we might have been better off without our juvenile foibles and pratfalls, positive nostalgia is not a fairy tale; at best, it is a romantic comedy, in which happy endings are paid for with ambiguity, conflict and complication.

While positive nostalgia always looks back with happy thoughts derived from longing, it should not always be construed as an affirmative response to life. It can also be an indirect expression of fear and uncertainty. My first bout of positive nostalgia came in the last six weeks of sixth grade, when I was 12 years old. With the end of the term looming, I anticipated leaving a school where I had been a student for four years and exchanging a familiar paradigm—a simple one-room class with one set of pupils—for a strange and complicated one—a daunting secondary school, with multiple rooms and hundreds of mingling students.

With each passing week that spring, I looked back on the weeks that came before, reflecting on how great they had been. Every moment now irretrievably gone seemed so much better than what I experienced in the present and faced in the future. I mulled in exquisite detail activities and events of recent weeks that had been unremarkable and mundane but which seemed enchanted in retrospect, since they were farther from the dreaded end of term than where I found myself. I wished to drift into the past and stay there, so I would never have to confront the cataclysmic changes that lay ahead. Only the end-of-year picnic, where I received a black eye in a fight, helped me shake off my nostalgia.

Parenthood is one life experience that seems exempt from nostalgia. Though I have been a parent for much of my adult life, and reflect fondly on many times in my daughter's growing up, I am not nostalgic about raising her. Is parenthood nostalgia-proof? Perhaps like childbirth, child rearing is so fraught that one only recalls the highlights and forgets everything else.

Reminiscing about the peak moments of my daughter's childhood and teen years makes me happy but not wistful. The experience was rewarding, yet I don't wish to relive it. Parenting is also nostalgia-free because it is never fully in the moment, but a forward-looking process. Looking back with dewy eyes at a past milestone might have put my daughter in a freeze-frame and depreciated her subsequent progress.

Positive nostalgia is a pervasive but not universal phenomenon. A significant number of people recall the past without longing or affection. Many shrug at the good times they never had. They shudder at setbacks, mishaps and disasters they endured, and sigh in relief that the past is a place sealed off to which they will never return. These individuals may not enjoy the present or anticipate the future but they will not wallow in the quagmire of the past, which they have mercifully forgotten or therapeutically repressed. Yet despite their coping tactics, even such haters of yesteryear cannot escape the insidious reach of nostalgia. Theirs is simply a different type, a *negative* nostalgia.

Negative nostalgia is an emotional state I've personally experienced. When people speak or sing about their fond memories of youth and a glorious past, admittedly a coral structure of living fantasies constructed of empty shells, I have nothing to contribute.

When I reflect on my distant past—teens and early years, the ripest time for nostalgia to feast upon—I have manifold memories but few good ones. I can replay many scenes from my early 20s but they can mostly be summarized in four words—struggle, frustration, hope and disappointment. Yet I too have been susceptible to nostalgia, not for what happened, but for what I wished had happened and never did.

Negative nostalgia, the longing for what never was, is not a reconstruction or memory, but a tortured attempt to *synthetically* construct an emotion, connection, or fulfillment one never experienced. A person with negative nostalgia must be an emotional chemist, producing artificial flavors without tasting the original ones. Contemplating an empty space and attempting to fill it can be a painful endeavor. What we missed in life may have a more potent impact than what we had and lost. Longing intensifies our desire for missing objects and imagination enhances their reality. This is the essence of negative nostalgia and why it can lead to madness.

While negative nostalgia induces a craving for what is not and has never been, it can also shut off a desire for what might be. While you bang on locked doors of the past for what you lost or never had—a loving parent, a satisfying friendship or an enthralling romance—you become oblivious to present possibilities. If you had a poor relationship with your father, you may mistrust all male authority figures. Rather than enlist mentors, you make enemies. If you lacked a nurturing family life when you were growing up you might reject family life as an unnecessary burden.

Negative nostalgia breeds a sense of isolation and makes the world seem alien. Holidays and other occasions for groups to gather and bond are always for others, and never for you. While you may derive strength from being an outsider for a while, you come to realize despite yourself that you are missing something you deeply want, which is stronger than your resistance. At last, you reach for what you never had, but too late—negative nostalgia has deprived you of the objects of desire and the skills to obtain them.

Many people are resigned to indulging negative nostalgia in recurrent daydreams, while others simply experience it as a restless, inarticulate pining. Still others attempt to act on it. The prototype for negative nostalgia in action was Don Quixote. The Knight of the Woeful Countenance pored over tales of chivalry. Without a concrete notion of how knights lived, or a plausible context for knighthood, he mounted a nag, wore a shaving pot on his head, and set out to do deeds of derring-do, such as jousting with a windmill and making courtly love to a prostitute. For a Russian twist on negative nostalgia, Anton Chekhov's *Three Sisters*, *Uncle Vanya*, *The Seagull* and *The Cherry Orchard* present a gallery of thwarted souls who pine for experiences, desires and lovers they never had and never will.

The "bucket list" is today's version of acting on negative nostalgia. It conveys the grief of having never done what one wanted most to do. But rather than carry this deprivation to the grave, we may do the thing we wanted to do and fill the void of missing out. The "bucket list" gives negative nostalgia a happy ending. It suggests that there is no statute of limitations on obtaining what one never had.

Negative nostalgia can be a steep and slippery slope. Once you pine for one experience you never had, the imagination may wander and desires can run amok, replicating uncontrollably. Today you may resent never going to Hawaii, while tomorrow you're booking a charter to Easter Island. Or missing out on skiing might snowball into negative nostalgia about not making the Olympic team, which could avalanche into a hopeless longing for a gold medal. It goes downhill from there.

Negative nostalgia may appear sterile, empty and circular—an internal mechanism that loops back to the bitter longing that triggered it. Perhaps it is this way for our own protection, like the body paralysis we experience when we're asleep that keeps us safe in bed when we dream. If, for instance, I were to act on my negative nostalgia for skiing, having never been on skis, I might crash into a tree. Since fulfilling a negative nostalgia is implausible and even dangerous, it can seem pointless and self-defeating. It could be called "Miniver Cheevy Disease," after the Edward Arlington Robinson character who fantasized about doing great things as he drank himself into a stupor.

Hardcore realists may scoff at negative nostalgia for affixing itself to deeds never done, places unseen and emotions neither requited nor shared, yet such a dismissive response reflects a literal physical interpretation of human experience. There are many ways to know or feel beyond the boundaries of fact and sensation. Just because I have never done, perceived or felt something does not preclude me from experiencing it in my mind, which is the origin and destination of all feelings and sensations. Desire is a way of knowing things; imagination is another. Often, these two mental operations coincide and collaborate to provide our most powerful and enduring experiences.

The quintessence of negative nostalgia is to know and desire a thing one has never had in such rich detail that it seems palpable, yet to be unable to find its equivalent in the physical world. Into this discrepancy slip the emptiness and longing.

A third strain of nostalgia, no doubt its prototype, is still going strong.

Saudade (SO DOD JAY) is a free-floating and wistful nostalgia that originated in Portugal. *Saudade* at first signified a feeling of loss, which widows and orphans of missing sailors experienced when their intrepid husbands and fathers did not return from the sea. But over time *saudade* evolved into a national and then international neurosis. It even has its own Brazilian holiday (January 30, if you wish to circle it on your calendar).

If positive nostalgia is like osteoarthritis of the psyche, an emotional condition associated with creaky age and manifesting in a longing for the joy and vigor of youth, *saudade* is like fibromyalgia of the soul, an elusive sensibility that causes pain and anguish for what is, for what is missed, and for what can never be.

Saudade started as "the love that stayed when someone was gone"—a contemplation of emotions and experiences associated with a person or place that induced joy—and a lingering emptiness and pain because that person, place or activity was lost. Yet, *saudade*, like irony, graduated from a feeling about one thing to an attitude about all things, a permanent and free-floating sense of loss that never quits, an insatiable longing for completion.

Saudade is more common and universal than one might think. The Brazilians and Portuguese have explored it but, like other emotions, it doesn't need a passport. Nor does *saudade* discriminate in age or gender. Youth is as susceptible to this insidious nostalgia as maturity. For instance, when I was in my late teens and early 20s, I loved parties. Yet regardless of how much I enjoyed a party, I often felt despondent when it was over. I missed the great moment and knew I could never have it back. I experienced *saudade* for the party without knowing what it was.

Like negative nostalgia, which is derived from it, *saudade* can also be aroused by objects one never had and by a striving for connection. When I was 19 years old, I walked alone in Paris at rush hour. My mind was dilated, my imagination inflamed by the many people streaming from work and striding to evening destinations, chatting or window-shopping with meditative faces. I wanted to meet them all, swallow their lives whole, and inhabit their worlds. Yet, I knew it was impossible. Rather than embrace this desire to be one with humanity, as Walt Whitman did in "Crossing Brooklyn

Ferry," I desponded. That's *saudade*.

Saudade is the subject of many popular Brazilian songs. It even inspired a style of music, *Bossa Nova*. If Antonio Carlos Jobim was the Beethoven of *saudade*, "The Girl from Ipanema" was its Ninth Symphony. This song is about love that is tenderly felt but never shared. As the singer describes in affectionate detail the girl who strolls down the beach, he knows with every wistful line and lilting musical phrase that he will never even speak to her, not because he lacks the words, but because she will not hear them.

The Portuguese and Brazilians have studied this sweet, painful sensation but other nations have it too. The Bacharach/David tune *Always Something There to Remind Me* expresses the hunger for ghostly delight. Wherever the singer goes, he sees his departed lover. "How can I forget you when there is always something there to remind me." The French song *Autumn Leaves* is an exquisite homage to *saudade*. Falling leaves remind the singer of a summer love that is gone—the red leaves of her lips, the golden leaves of her hands. He misses her always but in particular when leaves fall. Love's evanescence and the ineluctable passage of time are rich veins of *saudade*.

In literature, *saudade* notably appears in early 20th century Dublin. In James Joyce's *The Dead*, Gretta Conroy hears a tragic Irish song at a Christmas party that awakens *saudade* in her for a pure and passionate love she was too young and conventional to accept. In the French new wave film *The Umbrellas of Cherbourg* two young lovers, separated by war and circumstance, encounter one another again, years after their relationship faded to black. In the final scene, they meet by coincidence, share a look, barely a glance, a split second soupçon of mutual recognition, of *saudade*, before the intervening time and their divergent fates wash over them and they revert to their lives as strangers.

Nostalgia is a longing for what we have known and loved, for what we wanted and never had, and most cruelly for what we wished to be but never were. It is the love that remains when a precious person, place, thing or vision is gone and it is the plangent clang of eternal loss from which there is no escape, since the beloved object can only be kept alive as an elegiac memory.

41

Yet nostalgia can also be a cascade of recollections that makes one feel more alive. It is a longing for home, connection and wholeness, for the beginning to which we will return for a new and better start. Nostalgia is also the paradise we imagine to have existed in a mythical golden age when we were a more innocent version of ourselves.

While this compelling desire cannot revive or restore the past, it provides a framework of an experience that has been hollowed out by time and forgetfulness only to be filled by our imagination. Nostalgia transforms the past into a beautiful seashell.

Amnesia and senility may be the only antidotes to nostalgia. Yet, nostalgia, despite its distortions and delusions, represents a genuine aspiration for fulfillment. It is the contemplation of something precious and inaccessible, the source of life from which living, itself, can often sever us.

TALKING TO MYSELF & GETTING A GREAT RESPONSE

Idiosyncrasies grow on us like wrinkles or a peculiar gait, distinguishing us in others' eyes as well as our own. Yet even ostensibly antisocial habits may have redeeming properties. One such vilified behavior is talking to oneself. It is not the pathetic, depraved practice it has been purported to be, but a healthy and often instructive social alternative. I have talked to myself for years and no longer feel self-conscious about doing so. Rather, I justify self-talk as a moral and compassionate social gesture: by talking to myself, I relieve others of the onus of listening to me.

Self-talk was never a behavior I wished for or predicted for myself. To the contrary, it was a fate I was warned to avoid at all costs. My father talked to himself, a propensity my mother identified as a sign of mental illness, a status other aspects of his behavior confirmed.

I did not have the profile of a self-talker. I was neither reticent nor reclusive by nature, but when I was alone with my thoughts, I couldn't keep them locked in silence. If I maintained my own discreet counsel, I feared that the thoughts and phrases in my head would go unheard, which was far worse than being forgotten, and that my voice would change, not from high to low, as in adolescence, but from strong to faint, like a strangled whisper.

That was how my mother sounded as she aged and grew more inward in solitude. When I phoned her, she would answer after several rings, "Hello?" There was a tremulous question in her faint voice, as if she were unsure not only of who was calling, but also whether she could make a sound in reply. No. I preferred to hear myself think aloud than allow my voice to be buried in my throat.

The congress of mind, mouth and ear that made talking to myself possible was no swift innovation but a slow accretion, a creeping evolution. I'd been thinking silently and discreetly for years, formulating questions, devising answers, composing sentences and crafting paragraphs in my head. Ideas swirled like spirits in an enchanted bottle, unable to take form in speech and differentiate themselves.

Such expressions dwelling in cerebral silence needed to be spoken and heard. They banged their tin cups against their cell walls in my maximum security cortex, crying, "Let us out or we will die!"

Thinking is the work of consciousness and speech is how we reinforce the thought, give it air, strike it like a match against the ear and ignite its blaze.

I might have been unaware of it for some time because, like many developments, it accrued furtively. How long had my lips been moving with a rolling freight of internal thought? But suddenly something was amiss. I was disoriented as if waking from a nap, when the only proof that I'd been sleeping was that I could not recall my last thought.

My first clear contact with "the other" inside me, *myself,* was in an empty locker room. I was changing for my workout and feeling sullen and oppressed. The imminent exercise did not faze me—I was used to it—but the routine, itself, felt like a ton on top of me.

I was thinking silently when I became aware that I had shattered the wall between thought and speech, between internal monologue and a dialogue with another entity. I knew this because I received a response.

"I shouldn't feel so tired," I complained. "I haven't done anything."

"It's tedious because you're always alone," I answered.

"Physical exercise isn't a party," I grumbled.

"But you don't have to walk around in a silent world," myself replied.

"There's no one here," I pointed out.

"What about me?"

"What about you? I don't know," I said. Was I having a breakdown? I glanced around the locker room. "People already think I'm strange. How much more alienation can I take?"

"A lot," my self replied, "You were made for it."

I chuckled. It was sadly true. This repartée was fun. But it was happening too fast. "Look, I don't like where this is going," I told myself. "I mean, you may be better than silent rumination or prattle with dull people. But if I start...I could become...a troll who walks around mumbling with hand gestures."

My self laughed. "You're already there."

I laughed robustly in response to my self's astute summary of my life and psyche. He clearly had inside information.

As I guffawed, the only other man in the locker room emerged and walked toward the showers. He was prancing naked after his workout, as he often did. He gave me an acrid look, since he believed I was laughing at him. When he passed I resumed my internal conversation.

"Okay, you know me," I told myself, "But If I cross this Rubicon without caring how it looks, I'll be flipping society the bird. It's like public lewdness."

"Life is short," my self observed wryly. "Take what you can get."

The conversation ended. I had given myself, or vice versa, something to think—and talk—about. It was a humbling circumstance given what I had aspired to be.

"You, the great orator reduced to an audience of one!" I groused as I went for my swim. I shook my head and smiled. I felt better, after all.

I didn't accept my taboo with an open mind and mouth. "I don't need more eccentricities," I told myself as if I were on a psychic diet. When the other voice had leaped from my unconscious and I became two parties in a dialogue, I was caught off guard, but now I knew it was there and I resisted it.

The personal stakes were high. Self-talking was a serious affliction, as well as a social transgression. I'd be declaring myself a pathetic misfit, a reject, a demented soul society would shun like a medieval heretic and from whom others would recoil.

But my resistance weakened. I saw that by talking to myself, I could accomplish two tasks at once—clarify my ideas and hear my voice. By speaking my mind, I could distinguish one thought from another and give each one its identity and permanence. My mouth would shape the words and my voice would resonate with articulate and cadenced sentences. I would never let it stifle and die in a hermit's whispers.

In time I made peace with this idiosyncrasy as I had done with my others. I analyzed it, made excuses for it and delineated its causes. Finally, I determined that talking to myself was a matter of emotional survival.

In my personal narrative, I was a wanderer in a wilderness who would feed on vermin and carcasses to slake starvation and catch hailstones in his mouth to avert deadly thirst. So what if I was using one part of my brain to hear another? Was it psychic cannibalism or a symbiosis to keep me alive? I told myself I was no cranky ogre but a human releasing enormous internal pressure.

For much of a typical day I was essentially alone. When I was in an office toiling before a computer screen, in a classroom expatiating to sulking students or in a conference room confounding inattentive colleagues with inappropriate conviction, I could not talk to them soul to soul with the same trust and intimacy I had with myself.

When Socrates said, "Know yourself," he was not suggesting that self-knowledge could be obtained by debating friends and tradespeople. One suspects that his most profound dialogues were those he conducted with himself before he toyed with the likes of Ion and Euthyphro.

We learn to be reticent with others to protect ourselves. If you speak candidly, you may put the soft underbelly of your soul in the open air for scavenger gossips to devour. For this reason, many who need to express and protect their intimate selves talk to therapists. But what is a therapist but an erudite and sympathetic listener who pledges to impart insight and coping strategies without judgment?

I do this for myself.

It's not that I have searching discussions with myself like a man haunted by an unborn twin merged with him in utero. I don't stroll arm in arm with an invisible me like two soul mates in one straightjacket. I am far more discreet than that.

Many may be offended by the description of a mosaic inner life. I write not to win them over but to comfort the ones who share this propensity with me, and for those who ache to open themselves to someone, who may even perish waiting for such a person to appear. These famished souls should be aware of the kindred spirit within.

Self-talkers don't deserve society's opprobrium. The persecution we receive contradicts the self-help, can-do, love-yourself culture in which we live. We make the best of what we have, and harm no one.

I was sitting in a café. My notebook was open but my pen was tapping the white page, not leaving a trail of ink on it. I looked around at the other customers, sipping, eating and chatting with one another in excessive bonhomie and animation.

Intermittently, I intercepted their pitying glances at the poor nebbish pretending to be a writer, struggling for purpose in his life. Then as if to kick psychological sand in my face, they increased their decibel levels.

"These *social animals* are so fake. And so proud of themselves," I muttered.

"You've got that right," myself suddenly chimed in. "They talk about where they bought smoked fish like they discovered the cure for cancer."

Myself and I chatted like this and the *social animals'* conversation went quiet. They glanced at me as if I were an outcast with a shopping cart, inflicting body odor on them.

"These *social animals* hate us," I told myself.

"Of course they do," myself agreed. "Enjoy it. You're winning."

"They look at me like I'm a freak, so how am I winning?"

"They've stopped talking because what you have threatens them."

"What I have?"

"A stimulating conversation, fool."

Suddenly, the group nearby moved to another unoccupied table across the room.

Competition is at the root of *social animals'* acute antagonism for self-talking. They believe their socializing is superior but if they were sure of it they would ignore the person chatting with himself.

Yet tolerant coexistence rarely exists. *Social animals* do not pity self-talkers; they envy and resent us *because* we enjoy our own company. It devalues their mingling. These *social animals* have bantered, babbled and gossiped their entire lives—and what do they get for their trouble but the obligation to pretend to listen to and care about what others have to say?

The *social animal* sees "the soul who selects his own society" at the next table having a lively conversation and protests, "It's not fair! I work at maintaining friendships and this lazy bastard talks to himself—and he's having a better time than I am!"

Social animals must punish self-talkers for their social anarchy and slacking. Their prestige is at stake. They will defend the boundaries of conduct and reaffirm what it means to be human. If being alone were fun, they maintain, no one would bother to be social.

"*Social animals* can deal with us in two ways," myself said. "They can include us or ostracize us. Ostracism is simpler, so they demonize us."

"That's right," I said as I fumed at the group of socializers who had moved away from me. "They disparage self-talking as deviant behavior like dumpster-eating and public excretion to reinforce conventional prejudices."

"They're trying to put us in a corner and make us suffer in silence."

We stopped talking to consider all of this as the social animals hastened out of the café, giving me one last disdainful glance on their way out.

"But scapegoating us makes no sense," I said. "It betrays their self-interest. Talking to myself is a civic virtue, like coughing in a handkerchief or covering a sneeze. It's an alternative to unwanted conversations."

"Exactly," myself agreed. "A person needs to talk but does it mean someone else must be forced to listen? Unsolicited chatter is a psychological assault, yet there is no legal protection from it. Bloviating isn't even considered mental cruelty."

Myself made a fair point. I had often wished that people who nattered about topics interesting only to themselves would practice restraint and discharge their volubility in a deserted field or an abandoned building. If such people talked to themselves, many would be spared their aggressive loquacity.

Self-talking may be repulsive to many, but others see it as a harbinger of mental illness. Some earnest and well-intentioned amateur shrinks in my life warned me that talking to myself could be construed as a sign of incipient psychosis.

At first I was caught between the perceived enmity of the *social animals* and the dire diagnosis of the amateur shrinks. Yet these two disparate camps concurred on one point—talking to myself was the pathetic outcome of my lack of social involvement. Even I recognized that I lacked the confidence or skill to talk to others and make friends.

However, what amateur psychiatrists diagnosed as mental illness was therapy for me. Talking to oneself was mental hygiene—an antidote to loneliness. I had often heard that to love life one had to love oneself. To become my best friend I needed to openly communicate.

Internal communication doesn't mean asking yourself how your day went or whispering, "Check out that woman at 2 o'clock!" You need to engage in genuine dialogue and find out what you feel. You need to share everything and hide nothing. Because who ought to know you better than yourself?

Self-talk turned out to have practical applications, as well. It offered good practice for talking to others and even for forming friendships. If I could be my own friend, perhaps I could befriend others.

It was also useful for rehearsing conventional conversation, in case I had an imminent job interview or a social function to attend. Regardless of what I wished to say, I might hear my tone and content before others did and determine if I liked the way I sounded. How many arguments have I avoided, how many feelings have I spared, by rehearsing what I said to myself before I said it to others?

I know solitary folks who will not talk to themselves for the same reason that others refuse to masturbate. They see it as a humiliating failure to do for themselves what they believe others ought to do with them. But such compunctions seem frivolous and self-defeating. People who do not talk aloud may lose their voices. When they hear themselves after long silences, they may sound strange to their own ears and to others, and grow more self-conscious and withdrawn.

Self-talk is not only a personal benefit and a social challenge, but also a practice. Self-talk has nuances and levels of proficiency. It also improves with familiarity. At first, I could only handle cheerful bromides, mollifying commiserations and rousing pep talks. However, I concluded that talking to myself would be a superficial bore if we always agreed or used our discussions only for mutual support. True harmony needs more than one voice and talking to myself was enhanced by multiple viewpoints. I evolved from a choir of self-affirmation to a give-and-take based on mutual trust and respect. Only then was I able to go from "Rah" Rah!" to "Ah hah!"

Gradually, I started to mentor myself. I gave myself perceptive explanations and prepared myself for a day's work, warning myself of potential pitfalls. I admonished myself to be calm before and after difficult encounters and reminded myself of past debacles. I was not one to chitchat with myself. I kept the communication illuminating and helpful. I tutored myself in the ways of the world, analyzing people's motives and relationships.

Eventually, I became more familiar with myself. I raised my voice in self-reproach, lambasting myself when I was foolish or blinded by egotism. I even called myself an "asshole" and insulted my intelligence. When you can execrate yourself, you know you have achieved a high degree of self-ease. When you can take criticism, and listen to name-calling and shouting from yourself without taking it personally or letting it ruin your relationship, you have achieved a high level of maturity.

The only rule of self-conversation holds true for all conversation:

there are no rules. There must be room for improvisation. At the same time, you need to be sensitive to your partner's needs. Sometimes you need to be a "yes man" to yourself, while at other times you need to simply listen. Meanwhile, on other occasions, you need to be the devil's advocate and the stern parent who pokes holes in delusional arguments.

I have explained self-talking to remove its stigma but I don't wish to give the misimpression that it's ideal or to be preferred to conventional socializing. I always wanted a normal social life, for people to listen to me and enjoy what I had to say. I even became a teacher in the belief that discussing interesting topics with captive students would provide the fulfilling interaction I craved. I was wrong.

Self-talking may be an occupational hazard of a communications career. When I am muttering on a street corner, the fear people have of me as they pass is palpable. They see me as a lost soul on the dark side of sanity and society.

Fortunately, my errant public behavior is camouflaged by today's technology. So many people amble down streets chatting on Bluetooth cell phones that one can't distinguish between cell-talkers and self-talkers. Now when I talk to myself it's unclear if I am on the cutting edge—or just on the edge.

Despite early misgivings, talking to myself went well for a while until it got complicated like any relationship. One day my self and I had a fight. I was fulminating about a trifling inconvenience or indignity when an internal voice snapped, "I've had it."

"Is that you? I mean, *me*?"

"I'm sick of it. You've been ranting for years. Grow up!"

"You're not supposed to criticize. You should be supportive."

"And we're supposed to give and take but I do all the taking. You wear me out. You're supposed to listen and learn, but all you do is talk."

"You're *me*. If I can't talk to you, who can I open up to?"

"You just vent. I can't be your sounding board anymore. Find something else to talk to, like your shoes or jacket."

"You *are* me! You can't refuse to listen."

"If I'm *you*, show some respect."

The voice went silent. I was stunned and chastened but soon dismissed the awkward clash as my mind playing tricks. Only later did I grasp what happened. I had been talking to myself, without considering that something *other* was inside me all along. Was the goal of self-talking to communicate with the other self?

The tone of my self-talking was transformed. This threshold event taught me that cursing myself was not a sign of self-love and that I should talk to myself with respect. Once I had a wider range of topics and the right tone, I could apply them to my social efforts with other people.

But this clash with myself suggested another interpretation. I needed to hear a new voice and viewpoint. So I started talking to my car. My old *Matrix* had been a good friend for over a decade. We'd gone 150,000 miles together. We'd both weathered storms—the car, literally so, as it was parked on the street. We had both been scratched, dented and cracked in our own ways.

My car, aka *Blue Matrix*, and I care for each other. I give it an oil change every 3,000 miles, which it appreciates, and if I can't afford to get it washed every week, it says not to worry—it will wait until the next rain shower to wash off the dust and bird droppings.

Blue Matrix has a gentle disposition and speaks in a voice like "Elmo" on "Sesame Street." Since it evokes a children show, I am much more decorous with this vintage jalopy than with myself. When it labors to change gears, I apologize for not getting it a transmission flush. I tell it not to strain its four cylinders because we're in no hurry. I will not curse, badger or belittle it. This is not only good manners but good sense. I don't want *Blue Matrix* to stall on a highway out of resentment or timidity.

I guess my car and the other objects I talk to these days are surrogates for myself. Yet this behavior reinforces my belief that all beings, including so-called inanimate things, have souls, even if they are souls we imbue them with.

It has become clear that the self-talking skills I developed could work in other social interactions but I have so few that this added benefit has gone unused.

Despite our most persistent efforts to avoid it, we are often alone. If you enjoy your own company, you may avoid the desperation that results in disappointing, even calamitous, relationships of convenience.

Nobody will ever know you like you know yourself, so why settle for talking to a stranger who doesn't know you when a more attentive and sympathetic ear is close by—your own? Myself and I are back together, stronger than before after what we've been through, and we can discuss anything openly and without judgment or remonstration.

You may conclude that by talking to myself I have palliated my loneliness without taking constructive steps to end it. However, I am not lonely. If I am often alone, it is because solitude is a benefit to writing and a burden I willingly bear. In any case, internal communication should not be viewed as a remedy at all but as a tool for self-discovery that I recommend to all artists who wish to know themselves better. Of course, myself does not concur. *He* thinks it may result in nothing more than an extended communion with the mirror.

TAKING THE STAGE

If you're lucky to live long enough you may not only see your old clothes come back in style but your old dreams and ambitions return to life.

When I was very young, before my voice broke and I entered high school, I wanted to be an actor. Why? Because I loved films and the screenwriter and director were rarely mentioned, except for a tortured Swede, a clever Frenchman or two and a few crazy Italians. They were behind the camera, whereas to my callow, young eyes, and to most audiences, as well, the important people were on the screen.

Actors received credit from me not only for their facial expressions, mannerisms, and the genius of their ambiguous, yet intense inner lives but for the words they spoke. In this sense, I was just a typical moviegoer, watching with a peculiar blindness.

In mass media what we perceive with our senses means more to us than what we imagine. While it is true that a clever person must write dialogue, the audience values it only when it is spoken. Since the audience can only focus on one person or thing at a time, we adulate the actor, who animates the words, attitudes and character written for him.

After starring in grade school theatricals, my early potential was stymied in junior high, where I received only supporting roles if I was lucky. In ninth grade I had to write my own play in order to be cast, and in high school, I received non-speaking parts. The end of my acting dream was drawing near.

Acting is like athletics in one key respect—regardless of what you think of your own talents, actual or potential, what others think of you is more important—because you have to audition and be chosen. Any objective look in the mirror told me that I did not possess an expressive face, a graceful body or remarkable stage presence. In addition to these deficits, I had a disqualifying tendency to squint under bright lights, which meant that I could only play characters who wore sunglasses. There was also something about me that induced drama teachers to cast me as fat men and muscle builders, despite my lanky build. Either my teachers saw with ruthless insight the comic possibilities of squeezing every incongruity from my improbable appearance, or I had been a corpulent person in a previous life and a fat aura continued to encircle my emaciation.

Instinctively I understood my niche and gravitated to the Theater of the Absurd, but that genre was already a relic when I came of age. In high school I received bit parts and backstage assignments and finally a non-speaking role for which I shuffled on and off a dark stage. My puerile calling to be an actor stopped calling. I found other outlets.

Except for a few later roles in student films, I retired my acting dream and made peace with it. Then one day, while teaching English, I read aloud a passage of *Death of a Salesman*. After I had recited the part of Willy Loman for ten minutes, a student asked if I had ever been an actor. "No!" I replied emphatically. "It's a shame," she said. "You missed your calling."

I shrugged off this incongruous praise without a tinge of regret.

However, years later, destiny transported me back to my childhood vocation. A production of my daughter's one-act play that was to be featured in a drama festival had suddenly lost a key actor. It was too late for my wife, the producer, to audition other actors and continue to rehearse so I agreed to step in. Since my wife was also the director, I was confident that I would have the best acting coach. I rehearsed diligently and learned my part as opening night loomed over me.

On one hand, this serendipitous opportunity was a vacation from my reclusive self. Typically, I tapped on a keyboard in solitude. My only interaction with others came when I was done and my only feedback came when I laughed at what I wrote. I was excited by the novelty of acting but I was also terrified of failing, not due to pride or self-esteem but responsibility. I had to do well for my wife's and daughter's sakes.

In particular, I wanted my wife, who had put her faith in me and spent so many hours coaching me, to be rewarded for her hard work and good will with a great production. I wanted to help her with her endeavor in the same way that she helped me with mine. I did not wish for a new career, to be discovered, or even to prove that my high school drama teacher had been wrong about my talent all along. My ego was not much engaged in this acting gig. My only ambition was to be good enough.

Before the first rehearsal, I spent a day running through my lines and developing the rudiments of a character. At that point, I saw what I was doing as a feat and a chore. I set the bar low. If I knew my lines and was not dreadful, it would be a small victory. That was all I thought I could manage and it seemed wise not to try for more.

Memorizing was the major impediment for me. I didn't think I could do it. But page-by-page I learned my part. With my wife's help I ran through the play 20 times that first day. When I went swimming, I practiced the part during my laps. Going over my lines would become part of my swimming routine even after the production was over.

A teacher once confided that many victories in writing come in revision—after the furious inspiration of the first draft has cooled. For a writer, the performance comes at the start, in the first draft, while revision comes later in thousands of calculations. In acting, the process is in reverse order—revisions come in rehearsal and the performance comes at the end. Performance is the objective toward which the actor strives and rehearsal is how he gets there.

The first rehearsal was my portal into the world of theater, when the project became fully real to me. My wife was discussing the play with another actor as he struggled to understand his character's feelings and motivations in a specific moment. In the quiet studio, the actor and director focused intensely on a character's intentions as if the fate of the world depended on them.

I realized then how serious the art and business of making drama real onstage could be. Energy, intuition and spontaneity were all required, and analysis, imagination and judgment, as well. The actor had to know at all times where he was in the play and to remember what he had to do, yet all such calculations had to be forgotten during the performance in order to make it authentic.

In rehearsal, I surpassed the "triumph" of knowing my lines and started to learn the strange and difficult craft of acting. I explored beyond the sketchy, first impressions I had formed of my character, which were useful in learning my part, and discovered that I did not need to adhere to these preliminary takes. My character was a palpable, living being I would create out of my instincts, experiences and understanding and bring forth into the fullness of existence in performance with other actors.

Each rehearsal meant more to me than an acting class. The other actors were colleagues *and* my first audience. They gave me the encouragement and affirmation I needed to believe in myself. By working with me and helping me to improve with each run-through, they let me know that they took what I was doing seriously and that I was giving them something to work with.

During each two-hour rehearsal, our ensemble of three ran through the play several times. It became clear to me that knowing my part was no longer sufficient. I had to know my character, the other characters, and the story. I also needed to be more in tune with the other actors.

I was fortunate that my two co-actors were happy and relieved by my first rehearsal performances. The actor I replaced had not been able to learn his lines and he did not understand the play, so my aptitude for memorization and interpretation gave me immediate value in my colleagues' eyes. This increased my confidence.

Finally, after a few weeks, I felt I knew my character, the other characters and the nuances of the play—the beats, the conflicts, the crises and realizations. I understood the other actors' intentions and we were working well together, connecting, not rushing through, but taking our time and enjoying each moment.

But in our last rehearsal I flubbed a few lines and my fragile self-belief was shaken. I believed I had made such progress. Was it an illusion? After a spate of beginner's-luck overachievement, I felt I was regressing. How could this be happening?

My wife's thespian wisdom saved me. She pointed out that losing the lines was a sign that I was in the moment. Now I needed to perform another trick of the acting craft. I had to maintain two levels of consciousness simultaneously—to lose myself in the moment while being conscious at all times of what was going on around me.

Our production was entered in a one-act festival but during our rehearsals it was an irrelevant afterthought. We deliberately blocked out the commercial context and end product of our endeavor in order to give our full energy and focus to the quality of our production.

However, a week before our opening night, we attended a producers' orientation meeting. The theater owner, who was the festival impresario, addressed 50 eager participants as he caressed his small dog. He was an actor who specialized in one-man shows, so he orated the house rules, the logistics of going on and off stage, and other technical requirements with pompous gravitas. Since the theater shared a hallway with a local Alcoholics Anonymous the festival director enjoined us to be "respectful" of his neighbors by not loitering and by being as quiet as possible.

The orientation meeting underscored the business side of this event. Thirty-six productions were entered in the festival and would be presented over three consecutive weeks. The winner of the competition, to be determined by audience ballots, would take home $1000. The message was clear: to *win*, we needed to do more than give the best performance of the best play. We were expected to promote ourselves and draw a massive audience. This arrangement favored a play with a large cast with large families and many friends who would pay $20 per ticket.

The producers' meeting was an exasperating primer in the exploitive reality encompassing our venture. Each of the 36 producers paid $175 to participate in the festival, so the theater owner would gross $6,300 even if no one attended the event. Each play was shown for three nights, in one of three nightly shifts. If an average of 25 people attended every performance, the theater owner could net almost $20,000. Meanwhile, the producers paid the cost of rehearsals and printing flyers and programs.

58

Our small troupe had already overcome challenges and started to believe in what we were doing. Now we were exhorted to consider our production in commercial terms, which vitiated and complicated our efforts. Doing a good play with only a handful of rehearsals was hard enough without the distraction of publicity and prizes. After the meeting, my wife and I resolved to devote as much time and money as needed to produce a moving theater experience and to ignore the competition.

The day of the dress rehearsal was the most nervous of my life. I kept my activities as normal as possible: I swam, took a steam and had coffee. Yet at every moment, no matter where I turned, I faced a major trial of my life—to act onstage for strangers. There would be no paying audience that night but each ensemble would perform for the theater owner and the producers, directors and casts of the other productions. A DVD was also being made of that performance, so it was the one for posterity.

In the subway to the theater, a fellow passenger was transfixed by me—no doubt because I was mumbling my lines. I went over my part relentlessly as I did before all rehearsals, but the woman's stare made me forget my lines. I viewed her presence in our train car as a bad omen but luckily she got off after a few stops, allowing me to refocus. We left the train at 42nd Street, stopped by a drug store and bought a bottle of water.

For the next hour until we went on, I was swimming in adrenaline and my body was poised to explode. My wife advised me to close my eyes and inhale for a count of four, hold for a count of four, and exhale for a count of four to slow myself down internally. As I waited for my cue outside the curtain, I thought, "If I can get through the first speech, I'll be fine."

I lumbered onto the stage and shouted hoarsely. Fortunately, my character was tired, agitated and disoriented, so I was remarkably real.

I made it through the first half of the play without so much as a pause, yet at each moment I felt that I held the entire weight of the play on my every word and gesture and that it would all collapse if I faltered. At one point I simply forgot the last line of a short speech. It was a cue for the other actor. He paused, waiting for me to say it and when I didn't, he did his next line regardless. I only realized it afterward but it spurred me to be more alert and the rest of the play went without a hitch.

"I was so proud of you," my wife exulted. It was what I wanted most to hear and I took her praise to heart because I knew I'd done well. We had our own small cast party that night. The next day we were off.

That Friday was opening night and I was a jittery mess. The open dress rehearsal was supposed to inoculate me against stage fright but I realized with chagrin that each performance was a new travail for a different audience. Again, I anxiously awaited my sound cue to enter stage right but could not hear it well, so I bounded on. That night, awkwardness and insecurity were my greatest allies. I used my nervousness to remain alert and convey my character's anguish and confusion.

With two successful renditions behind me and only one performance left to give, I ought to have been confident. Yet I had trepidations about the final night because my daughter, the playwright, would be in the audience with her friends. I could not sleep the night before. Then for the entire day of the show, we drove to and from her campus, a 200-mile round trip, packing and unpacking a carload of her personal effects. An hour before my ultimate performance, I ran through the play with my wife and blew a few lines. "I'm too tired, I can't do this!" I cried.

"Don't give yourself an out," she replied firmly. "Of course, you can do it. Take a shower and we'll run through it again."

That evening, I camped out in the men's room with my first nervous stomach. I was so hyper that I paced the hallway for 15 minutes, right to the door of the AA meeting and back, as I repeated my wife's breathing exercise with my eyes closed. My cast mates asked if I was okay. I was too abashed to tell them how sick I felt and didn't want them to worry.

Despite my preliminary nerves, the last show was our best. A full house and attentive audience inspired me to tell the story of the play to anyone who had not seen it. More than this, I wished to bring to life for my daughter's eyes and ears her words and vision.

The first review I received was promising. My daughter did not look mortified by my acting. After the show, she and her friends crowded around me and said how much they enjoyed my acting debut. My daughter was beaming. It was the first time she had seen her work onstage so I was relieved that she was proud of how it turned out, and that her friends approved of it. A few people I had invited also praised me. They were surprised I never acted before. "I had a great director," I told them.

For weeks after the festival, I regurgitated the play constantly and compulsively in my mind—even when swimming underwater—as if I expected the production to move to Broadway. When anyone uttered a remark to which one of my lines comprised an apt rejoinder, I delivered it.

However, my last performance was not the happy ending to this theater story. The real story only started with this limited engagement, which was not only *limited* by the number of days but by my acting aptitude and interest.

My wife, however, had no such limitations. Her talent, enthusiasm and commitment to acting were strong and genuine. I had no grand aspirations but my willingness to learn and fail showed her that she had nothing to fear by returning to her vocation and the actor's lot of auditions, roles, rehearsals and the company of directors and actors.

"You're the one who should be doing this," I admonished her. I encouraged my wife to audition and for several months I drove her to auditions all over town. Starting is always an ordeal, so I wanted to give her moral support, while making the process easier and more pleasant. Four months later, she had her first theater role. Within a year of her comeback, she was in two productions. After three years, she was in a web series, a short film and several theater pieces.

This was the best result I might have wished for from "strutting and fretting my hour on the stage." I had felt guilty for years that my wife sacrificed her dream for a day job and motherhood. Though I could never restore the time she lost, I might help her belatedly pursue her beloved art and vocation—with a greater appreciation for her ability, her knowledge and her love of acting.

AGEISM AND THE GOLDEN BOUGH

Ageism may be biologically determined. In procreative terms, older people are unnecessary for the perpetuation of the species. They are detritus. The attitude of society is, "Move aside, Clyde!"

As I get older I find myself excluded from the business of living. I'm treated as if life has only passing interest for me because I'm transitional, not fully part of the world. I am expected to be silent but even when I speak it doesn't matter, since no one listens. I fade into a spectral state.

I am kept at a deferential distance so that I may contemplate my final and most conspicuous life option—death—which I am expected to face alone, as I have faced most vicissitudes in life. It seems widely assumed that since I'm closer to death, I must be less alive. People, individually and collectively, do their part to induce me not only to contemplate death but to welcome it.

Humans need work. Being busy is our most natural state and we exert ourselves instinctively, turning even pastimes into labors of love. When we are deprived of purpose or subverted in our objectives, e.g. digging a ditch only to be forced to fill it, we lose our grip. For this reason, ageism is most cruelly asserted, effectively implemented and harshly felt in the workplace.

Yet favoring youth and eliminating age in employment, albeit perverse and illegal, may be hard-wired in our psyches. Despite our cultural evolution as a society of democratic institutions—rights over might and intellect over brawn—our species is stuck on biologically driven attitudes.

The discrimination mature professionals encounter may be a symbolic update of the transfer of power described in *The Golden Bough*, in which an aging king was murdered by his son in a rite of succession. Patricide was an ineluctable threshold event in tribal culture. Since older men could neither work as needed nor relinquish authority on their own, a ritual needed to be devised to execute and legitimize succession.

In a white-collar world, physical strength is irrelevant; yet the primal imperative for generational change is transposed on a cerebral culture that no longer requires it. Arbitrary age cut-offs frustrate older and more experienced job seekers because they seem gratuitous and run against our grain of fairness, justice and "common sense."

Systemic ageism is a poor business policy in any industry where experience counts. This is especially true in marketing and advertising. Are 20-somethings more qualified than 50-somethings to sell cars or pills to the old and the aged? It is unlikely that parents listen to their children more than their children listen to them.

Thanatos is the death instinct, the obverse of *eros*, or sexual love. Intuitively and empirically, humans know we change form and return to the earth. We all die but we don't want to know the details, to be told when the *coup de grace* will come or to be pushed into our graves.

Yet manufacturers and their advertising vendors will not accommodate us. Their motivation to sell products for our debility and demise outstrips their decorum. They have borrowed the Boy Scouts maxim, "Be prepared!" and are shouting it at our rapidly aging population.

A senescent generation now hears messages of *Thanatos* and is being prepped and programmed for a timely, orderly decline and death. Meanwhile, our legal and religious institutions maintain unequivocally that euthanasia and suicide are illegal and immoral. It's a perfect irony: we can sell painkillers to seniors but not put them out of their misery.

We face mass-*Thanatos*. The plan is simple: prevent older people from finding work, make them expend their entire equity, and when they are reduced to physical, emotional and financial husks, dispose of them. As worms recycle their flesh and bones, the banks will recycle their assets.

It is not a bizarre or novel idea. In Aldous Huxley's *Brave New World*, wretched characters who experienced old age spent their last days hallucinating on "soma." And in *Wild in the Streets*, a classic youth film of the 1960s, a rock star led a youth revolution, rounded up anyone over 30 and subjected them to a "cool" final solution: they wandered around geriatric camps wearing shrouds and tripping out in LSD oblivion.

When all the aging Baby Boomers collect their Social Security and our national treasury takes the hit, *Wild in the Streets* may offer younger generations a way out of the pit of debt.

But ageism is not just for the aged. You may not be young enough to avoid the cold fact that from the time you get too smart to make an impulsive purchase, marketers pander to your fear of infirmity and death. This indoctrination doesn't start at 40. I received my first junk mail from a mausoleum when I was 35. No wonder I became a morbid mess.

Mortality was a depressing fact I learned at an early age; poverty was another. While death made life feel painfully precious; poverty made it seem brutally cheap. This viselike paradox crushes the soul.

I often cursed poverty when I was young, but I'm grateful now that I had the precocious opportunity to practice being powerless and voiceless. Poverty was the apposite preparation for ageism—the poor person and the senior citizen are both visible beings rendered invisible by preterition.

A retired professor lives in my building. He was once the most vigorous and convivial of men. Now he's in his late eighties. Recently I saw him while we collected our mail. He was in his robe and slippers.

When I asked him how he was, he tilted his head and paused, as if his brain were a bomb on a timer. He seemed to have prepared and rehearsed a response for the first person who asked him this facile question.

"It is an unusual sensation," he confided, "to wake up each morning and have no reason to get out of bed." He regarded me intently to gauge my response and smiled with furtive satisfaction at the gravid effect he had. "You think, '*What's the use?*' Can you imagine that?"

"No," I replied. "I've never been that depressed."

The professor's lugubrious eyes and deep sigh acknowledged that I was better off not fully grasping his state of mind.

"I suppose it *is* depressing," he conceded with a shrug before adding with the lightness of a Viennese roast, "but that's how it is."

This exchange of ideas seemed to perk up the professor-emeritus because there was more speed in his shuffle as he carried his mail to the elevator. Having revived his didactic self, I wondered if there was an on-line service or hotline that might employ his ancient wisdom.

THE CREATIVE SPARK & THE COMPETITIVE FIRE

Competition and creativity do not mix well, except in a popular performance art form, like tap dance, in which the dancers have a tradition of "putting something on" one another. To perform well in most art forms, you need to stop thinking about what the next person does. When you turn your head, you lose. This is the true meaning of Lot and his wife, and of Orpheus and Eurydice. These tales signify what can happen when we lose faith and focus by looking back, rather than straight ahead.

If "beating" another writer is your motivation, your work reflects it. It does not stand distinctly on its own but has a mosaic quality. One can sense the presence of your competitor in everything you do. Conversely, if you view what you do as the expression of something intrinsic to you and to no one else, your originality will also be borne out in your work.

When I was in college, Ken Kesey, the author of *One Flew Over the Cuckoo's Nest*, dropped in on our fiction workshop while my story was being discussed. Afterward, Kesey said he liked my work but thought my writing was "too competitive."

Kesey advised me to remove my ego from the creative act and become one with my writing, as in *Zen and the Art of Archery*: only when I stopped trying, he said, would my efforts hit the mark. In another time and place, also *à propos* of writing, Gertrude Stein concurred in her own aphoristic manner when she said, "To try is to die."

Unfortunately, competition in writing has become more pervasive. There are extrinsic economic reasons for this. Contests and awards are touted as the best means for unknown writers to gain readership and credibility. Although awards and competitions quantify creative work, which is inherently unquantifiable, they also conveniently disqualify writers and artists who do not win the awards.

Contests and awards raise more questions than they answer: who are the judges and what are their qualifications, tastes and affiliations—professional and personal? Ultimately, most contests provide the greatest benefit to the sponsors and judges, which is why some institutions run awards throughout the year. Ironically, so many contests and awards currently exist that they lack the credibility to legitimate the winning writers.

Although I was always agnostic about the validity of writing competitions, I believed that someone must hold them in esteem, if no one else, then at least the judges who sifted through applications and supporting documents and sat in committees through arduous meetings as they fervently hashed out the most deserving applicants.

One evening, when I took out the trash for recycling, I found an intriguing stack of stapled sheets on top of the paper bin. A neighbor had disposed of a cache of documents. The top sheets were scoring forms for a highly coveted and competitive writing fellowship, on a niche below the MacArthur Genius grants.

As I flipped casually through these stapled applications, I surmised that they were confidential. Yet how private could they be if they were in an open wastebasket? I recognized some names on the coversheets. These were contest submissions in behalf of the most famous writers of a new generation. The packets contained recommendations from teachers, colleagues and other writers. A cursory glance told me they were full of lush metaphors and hyperboles.

I expected these applications to summarize and extol the candidates' work, yet few recommendations mentioned writing at all. Rather, the nominators conveyed their nominees' intangible non-writing credentials. Most underscored the writers' personal virtues, ("E—has written less than she might have because she teaches reading to developmentally challenged inmates in a correctional facility..."), or how much they suffered for their art, ("Despite being a three-time finalist for the Fennimore Prize for Emerging Voices, B—has been homeless and eating out of dumpsters...").

Such entries suggested that writing was a brutal and grueling art and that putting words on a page was only part of a writer's vocation. The self-immolating exploits of these contesting literati reminded me of the performance artist Chris Burden who had his arm shot and his hands

66

hammered by nails as exhibits of his performance art. Yet, despite the vaunted literary attainments and desperate heroics of these lofty aspirants, their applications lay in our recycling bin—as unshredded refuse.

These processed fellowship applications exposed the incongruity of competition and creativity. They were clearly grist for a tedious, arbitrary and political process resembling college admissions. Their haphazard disposal also put the neighbor who discarded them in a dark light, as a connected and cynical critic who did not respect the power he held or the people it affected. I wondered if I should approach him or shun him.

Apparently, the only effect competition had on creative writing was to give "winners" the ephemeral encouragement that their efforts were loved by someone, somewhere, sometime. For this fleeting kiss of approval, which many might mistake for lifelong bliss and Best Seller Lists, writers would continue to send their money and their work to dubious contests.

In this way, competition beguiles millions of souls to chase after what 99% will never get while misleading everyone into a wasteland where creativity loses significance. Meanwhile, most honors and awards that contests bestow are like the money people carried in wheelbarrows during the Articles of Confederation—worthless paper few recognize or accredit.

Regarding the awkward relationship of creativity and competition, I reflected on a passage in *On the Duty of Civil Disobedience* by Henry David Thoreau. It seems to define the raison d'être of creativity and its place in the human psyche:

"When an acorn and a chestnut fall side by side, the one does not remain inert to make way for the other, but both obey their own laws, and spring and grow and flourish as best they can...If a plant cannot live according to its nature, it dies; and so a man."

Each of us creates according to our individual talent, viewpoint and experience. Regardless of whether or not a writer is acclaimed, if he loves writing and loves what he produces, he has succeeded in such a manner that no one can ever diminish his accomplishment.

THE 365-DAY VACATION

One disappointing myth of American life is the vacation. A working person flees his routine for two weeks to forget the tedium of the other 50. The outcome of time off is often the opposite of its intent: people return to brutish servitude as exhausted and dispirited as when they left, feeling more cheated and deprived than ever.

This perplexing, self-negating rite is rooted in a conspiracy of opposites—reward *and* punishment. Work is compensated with a desired object—freedom and enjoyment—to reinforce the primacy of *work*. A vacation is either so restorative that it motivates us to earn another one or it extends the drudgery so that we want to rush back to our coarse grind.

Friedrich Nietzsche was the first to note the chicanery inherent in time off. In *Beyond Good and Evil* he quipped that English Sundays were deliberately boring breaks so people would be eager to work on Monday.

Vacations don't often work out as planned because they follow the pattern of employment. Most people take holidays at the same time. Instead of the daily commute to our place of business, we fill the same roads, rails and skies en route to paradise. We flee each other only to spend money in the same exotic climes.

Yet we are not "can't win for losing" victims of a cruel metaphysical hoax. We like our vacations this way and plan our breaks for when other people take them, due to childish insecurity. We hate feeling left out or left behind. Taking time off at the same time gratifies our egalitarian need not to miss out. We want to be at least as good as everyone else.

Ironically, the luxury of doing things when others do them leads us down a twisted path to the toil we tried to escape. We "pack up all our cares and woes" but stress won't be denied; it comes along for the ride.

Imagine the photographs and videos we'll post on social media: being stuck in traffic, jostled in crowds, waiting in lines, getting spilled on and stepped on by others who are also grasping at the brass ring of a good time.

Most lives are not lived but endured. We know vacations may betray us but we covet them anyway. The imperative to escape work, flee our selves and cheat our routines is a universal yearning. It springs from the concept of paradise, which our ancestors have never lost in the vale of tears. When work is a curse and civilization is our discontent, vacations are the antidote to every ill and alienation.

Vacations are also a diversion from a greater freedom lost. According to Frederick Douglass, slave owners encouraged slaves to drink, play games and engage in obstreperous behavior during holidays in order to discharge and diffuse their restless energies in a controlled and self-destructive manner. After two weeks of idleness and dissipation, slaves were so sick and demoralized, Douglass wrote, that they gratefully embraced their servitude as a refuge from revelry.

Paid time off is a social escape valve for us, as well. However, it is also the only free time most working people get, save for long weekends and holidays, when we can shed business attire and experience our lives and ourselves as more than a sum of useful parts.

We have been taught that life is hard and dull and the sooner we adapt to it, the better off we'll be. We are resigned to punishing ourselves 96% of the time for the sweet 4% set aside to refresh our bodies and our minds. The typical vacation is an ephemeral heaven, but if we didn't go through hell to get there, we might not deserve a vacation—or need one.

Vacations identify us and mark our status. Where and how we spend our breaks say as much about us as where we live or how we get around. Time off punctuates time, differentiates our years and gives us matters to discuss, remember, dream about and compare our regular lives against.

The psychology of the vacation is a response to work but it is rooted in our experience of time, specifically, the present. Most people respond to "now" only as a point of comparison between past and future. They wish today were as good as "yesterday", or hope it will improve "tomorrow."

These people have "flexible selves' and they live in the "elastic present."

The *elastic present* is an ingenious feature of the human psyche that allows us to imagine ourselves backward and forward in time, expanding the present and extending ourselves beyond who and where we are at any moment. It is as if we wrapped our arms around our entire lives—past deeds, current circumstances and future hopes and plans—and carried them before us like great duffle bags.

However, the *elastic present* is not a psychological monopoly. Another attitude toward the present persists in those of us who believe that the past was not good enough to revisit and that the future is unlikely to improve on it. We live in the *eternal present*.

The *eternal present* is the oldest, most fundamental concept of time, from before our species knew what time was or had developed such mental accessories as history and hope. The present was once the Pangaea of time, a super-continent that seemed to go on forever, only riven by rivers of change and encircled by an ocean of death. The *eternal present* must have dominated the consciousness of our ancestors because surviving each day was not a dull given, but a harrowing ordeal.

As humans started to record and measure time, we whittled "now" into fragments, which grew smaller as our time-measurement became more precise. Our frequent psychic flights into the past and future have further splintered time into islands of the present that we pass over as we anticipate future events, like vacations, and reflect on milestones of the past. However, if we commit to living in the present, we may expand the atoll of "now" from a sliver of time back into a continent—or at least a spacious tract of our own.

Granted, living in the eternal present when everyday is trying, tiring and tedious is not an appealing proposition; to the contrary, it may feel like crossing a swamp. Most people might consider themselves better off by forging through each dreary day under general anesthesia or several analgesics, until they reach the next long weekend or holiday.

But what if we changed our concept of the vacation by incorporating into our eternal present the exotic, the curious, the desirable and the interesting? What if we added something new to the dreary sameness of every day and sprinkled big event enthusiasm onto our routine?

The difference between communication and chatter, or the one you know and the indistinct *other*, also exists between everyday—generic and featureless—and today—which is unique and vibrant with potential.

If the future looms as a forbidding frontier, and the past flashes across your memory as a bleak wasteland, and your present is all you have to work with or believe in, you may need a *365-Day Vacation*. The *365-Day Vacation* is not only a philosophical position, but a practical solution if a trip is beyond your means or if business suffers when you're gone. You may lack the stamina to plan or take a full vacation or you may have PVSD (post vacation stress disorder) just thinking about one. Flashbacks of bad vacations past may result in headaches, nightmares and night sweats. You may have premonitions of a vacation disaster or of your home being ransacked in your absence.

When such caveats cloud your spirit, you may opt for the *365-Day Vacation*. This is no misprint. Nor is it a grandiose prescription to stop working and live on the dole. The *365-Day Vacation* is a simple trick that requires only a change of attitude and a small effort to do something each day to satisfy your body or soul.

The *365-Day Vacation* ought not to be driven by compulsion, like the ritual of lunch, when we order meals that sap our energy and give us indigestion. It is to be celebrated in a creative act, a reflective moment or an aesthetic perception. Rather than a predetermined activity, like prayer or yoga, the *365-Day Vacation* is disbursed among a hundred small acts—stretching, conversing or listening to music. It is the same exhilaration promised by a two-week vacation sprinkled liberally over an expanse of ordinary days.

The concept of the *365-Day Vacation* first presented itself when I was giving personal English lessons to Sammy, a Chinese programmer. Sammy and I would go to a coffee shop and practice conversation. Sammy was an English beginner but he was so intelligent that words alone could not prevent him from communicating his ideas, regardless of their complexity. There were two details about Sammy I still recall: his T-shirt with a cartoon kitten and the words "Please like me" on his chest and his vacation theory.

Sammy maintained that life would get harder for people as time went on. They would be forced to work longer days and more weeks per year. Eventually, they would be too tired and too poor to go on vacation trips and would spend their precious time off resting at home.

My life already exemplified Sammy's grim forecast but it was too painful for me to acknowledge it. I still harbored the bourgeois dream of two-week vacations at a shore, on a mountain or in an exotic land. Yet like any truth, Sammy's theory of the restful *anti-vacation* was magnetic. It breached my psychic defenses, replicated in my mind, and became more real with every passing year.

A good while after I met Sammy, a variation of his concept resurfaced randomly while I played basketball with my university colleagues. One player of note was the dean, a thin, hunched and apparently unfit academic, who seemed more comfortable donning tweeds and stringy ties than shorts and sneakers.

Despite his sporting indifference for athletic competition, the dean endured my rugged defense and frequent fouls, made some shots and performed better than anyone expected he would. Yet when anyone complimented his play, the dean shrugged self-effacingly and insisted he had no athletic ability or skill.

But the dean wasn't modest or coy. He revealed an attitude toward our friendly game that was subversive of competition and heretical to sports lovers. He claimed that he wasn't trying to play well or even consciously exercising—he just let his body go and do what it wanted.

At first, I believed the dean was jesting until I realized that he was applying Sammy's theory of the *anti-vacation* to the basketball court. Unlike the other players in our pick-up game, dignified and respected men who briefly escaped their daily rigors by playing hard and re-enacting the competitive ardor of their youth, the dean recreated without escapism or exertion. Sport was not separate from his daily life, only a small part of it.

Then it dawned on me that with the right attitude, one might incorporate enjoyment and recreation into each day, without going too far or doing too much. It would be a small vacation—and a major victory: I would lead my own personal revolt against the deadening routine—no work, all play for a few moments every day.

So what does one do each day of a *365-Day Vacation*? No itinerary is required; to the contrary, it is discouraged. We're working with minutes, perhaps no more than an hour, so every moment must count. Yet, the paradox of transforming dull minutes into vacation oases is that one never feels pressed for time. Each moment that is not accounted for is like a gift basket that one feels free to fill with discovery and pleasure. When one wishes to savor one's freedom and time, pressure wanes. Where we go matters less than how we get there.

Even among those of us who take the *365-Day Vacation*, some have more panache than others. I once had a colleague who fit several vacations in a day. He began by biking early mornings to his local YMCA for a vigorous swim. Then he slept on the commuter train and took a three-mile hike from Grand Central Station to his downtown office. At lunch on a sunny afternoon, one found him basking on a bench in a playground in Little Italy. With legs stretched and eyes closed, he turned his face to the sun. In the evening, my colleague walked back to the station in waning daylight. Rest and exercise were key components of his *365-Day Vacation*, just as Sammy the Programmer had predicted. Did any South Beach beachcomber take more splendid advantage of his leisure than my epicurean colleague?

This man taught me more than anyone I met in my sequence of day jobs about maintaining one's dignity, humor, clarity of mind, tolerance and appreciation for the simple pleasures life provides. Many of his colleagues may have wondered how he managed to keep a job and survive given how much abuse he took, but it was no surprise to anyone who knew him well. His *365-Day Vacation* had refreshed him to such an extent that he could brush off life's insults and injuries like lint from his coat. He held his last job for 15 years before he retired.

Not many of us are as gifted as my former colleague in the fundamentals of living. We struggle with the banalities and petty affronts that are flung at us at every turn—street singers the surgeon general never issued warnings against; the hot air and brainless word fodder spewed around the radio dial; the entertainment void known as cable TV; and the political speeches and internet diatribes that take us to superfund toxic waste dumps of the mind and leave us there. Is it surprising that we grow inured to the gratification each moment offers?

For several years, I rarely left town on a vacation that did not involve visiting my in-laws. Adopting the *365-Day Vacation* was a necessity for me. I have since become proficient at carving an hour now and then out of my day to escape stress and drudgery. If the time spent makes me feel better, I call it time off, whereas if the time is full of toil and pressure, I call it work, even if I spend it thousands of miles away from an office in the shade of colossal palms. The key is not how our activity looks to others, which is our usual litmus, but how it feels while we're doing it.

If you intend to try the *365-Day Vacation*, you must be prepared for trial and error. Mistakes are inevitable as you learn what brings you peace and satisfaction. Finding activities and destinations that gratify without long lines is not a science. Such information can only be culled from experience, luck and a disposition to try. But once I find what I like, I repeat it, not everyday, which would diminish its luster, but often enough to make it a pleasant option. Over time, such recurrent pleasures become routines, then traditions.

Some readers may view the *365-Day Vacation* as a code or euphemism for long-term unemployment, a perception that is facile and false. Relaxation should not be mistaken for idleness or penury. Employment and unemployment are both stressors and miseries, and most people who have experienced both know full well that being out of work is no antidote to overworking, but a much harder job.

In any case, the *365-Day Vacation* can help you make the most of both circumstances.

For instance, I have been able to have micro-vacations in my low-partition cubicle by jotting down an intriguing idea or observation I had on the train, by stepping outside and walking down streets of interest, or by lounging on a park bench like my old colleague did, taking in the local people and basking in the sun. By the same token, when I have been knotted up and miserable over being unemployed, I have made vacation time between résumés and interviews to dip into my books and refresh my mind with philosophical or historical points that seem to belong to someone else's life but which for many years dominated mine.

I am reconciled to the possibility that the *365-Day Vacation* is unlikely to catch on like a new diet or a financial strategy people pore over on a commuter train. For one, the *365-Day Vacation* yields no bragging rights and confers no status. It is tantamount to cooking a delicious roast from a cheap cut of meat. It provides no content to discuss or post photographs about on social media, because it seems unimpressive, regardless of how good it is. You can't share it with those who may envy you but who will never hang out with you.

However, if your objective is to refresh, rather than impress, the *365-Day Vacation* has the right itinerary for you. The *365-Day Vacation* may lack far-flung adventure, attitude and edge, but it can keep you sane and fit. Today, when much of our food, water and air are tainted in diverse ways and travelers face disease and hatred across every border, "sane and fit" is a hard bargain to refuse. When you stay home you always go first-class. You also see more in a mirror than in a social media post.

MAXIMIZING PRODUCTIVITY IN WRITING

Writing is a practice strengthened by character. Talent is necessary, but to optimize your aptitude, you must be resourceful, accountable and consistent.

When I started writing, I always had reasons NOT to do it. Gradually, I developed discipline. Now it feels wrong if I don't write. Working with words is my refuge from uncertainty, anxiety and discomfort.

To make writing a strong and dependable part of your life, there are some character traits you will need to strengthen.

Resourcefulness.

I knew an artist near Taos, New Mexico who served guests cracklings made of fried pork blood. He said he used every part of the hog, like the Plains Indians did with the bison they slaughtered.

I have applied this ingenuity to my writing. I use everything, including fears, illnesses, inconveniences and poor sleep to help me write.

If I have no computer, I write by hand. No paper? No problem—I scrawl on my skin. If I can't sleep, I write until my eyes won't stay open. If I wake up prematurely, I get up and use the clarity of my racing mind.

In this way, I turn weakness to strength and build self-esteem. If I do nothing more that day, I am happy because I have already put in some work.

Time management. Expectation fulfillment.

A man I once met on the unemployment line asked me, "How do you know when you're working?"

"Is this a trick question?" I asked.

"I've always had jobs," he said. "I'm in an office eight hours a day and I know I'm working. But being a writer is unstructured, so how do you know you're working?"

It was a fair question, but I had an answer for it. When I made writing my vocation, I knew I had to account for my time and effort. It didn't matter to me what others thought of my career choice as long as I believed in myself and the sincerity of my commitment. I made sure I was working by recording the number of pages I wrote each day.

I still set daily goals for myself and make sure I meet them. This keeps me accountable, distinguishes one day from another and gives me a sense of progress. Without accountability, one day gets lost among the rest while the writing also gets lost in the business and disorder of living.

Consistency.

I knew a writer who wrote one hour per day. He claimed one hour was the ideal parcel of time in which to accomplish any project.

"Only an hour?" I scoffed. It sounded like an all-you-can-eat diet.

The "Man of the Hour" patiently explained that a year of hours "chunked together" equaled 15 days. While this sounded like a finger-snap, Jack Kerouac wrote a draft of *On the Road* in the same amount of time.

I did the math. Fifteen days equal 360 hours, or one hour per day for just under a year. If I stretched two weeks over 51 weeks and wrote for one hour a day, I might make significant progress under minimal pressure.

It was like "the spacing effect" in memory. Pacing my creativity would produce the best results, since it was easy to stay fresh and focused for an hour at a time. This ended my binge writing. I learned not to be greedy with inspiration, but to spread it out and keep some in reserve.

However, at times I got carried away and my brain overheated. It was dangerous. A hot brain felt euphoric, but it could also burn out.

"Stop writing," I told myself. "Step away from the desk. Take a walk." Writing for too long can be like writing drunk: you think you're in *the zone*, but it's only the Twilight Zone.

FAILURE

The Myth of Failure

Failure is like a mysterious disease—or a bad cold. No one can say where it came from, why you have it, what precisely to do about it or when it will leave. Yet once you feel it, you know there's no easy way out of it. All you can do is persevere and hope you're free of it sooner than later.

Although failure was a result I feared more than anything, I couldn't let it daunt me. I had to push forward and do what I felt was necessary to succeed. Yet while I tried to fend it off, failure was my constant companion, even before it brutally assaulted me. Failure goaded, tormented and jeered at me. The prospect of failure was terrifying—it signified the protracted torture of doing what I did not want to do and what no one else respected or cared about. It meant looking at myself in a mirror everyday knowing I had failed and having others look at me, knowing the same thing.

Most of all—and this was the worst of it—failure meant a tedious and worthless fate that was agony for me and beneath the notice and contempt of others. I had always believed that to be fully alive I needed to be the person I wished to be, to eagerly anticipate the coming day as though it bore the possibility of more success and fulfillment than I already had.

To fail was the opposite of this. It was to be incomplete, to have nothing to look forward to and nothing at stake. I would henceforth be inert as my life moved by, living out my years on Earth, rather than living them. While I experienced the worst agonies of failure, I believed I faced a life sentence and that my life was a prison camp. I lived but was only half-alive because I had committed the worst crime against myself—I failed to fulfill my expectations.

Yet while failure rode me bareback, its spurs biting into my brain, I believed my hopes and aspirations would be redeemed and that I would overcome the chaos and obscurity of the dismal present. I subsisted in the amniotic bubble of juvenile desire and swore allegiance to my talents. I reassured myself that I could "make it" and trusted my self-administered doses of encouragement because without them I had nothing but doubt, confusion and frustration.

The Pathogenesis of Failure

Before I was aware of being sick with failure, it loomed as a generic and remote possibility—like cancer, heart disease or a bad accident. It could happen to anyone—but it wouldn't happen to me.

I experienced failure in two principal ways. In the acute and active phase, my efforts were unavailing. What I had done before no longer worked. Prior successes turned to vinegar for reasons beyond my comprehension and control. This aspect of failure I internalized as deep frustration. Failure's second "chronic" phase comprised its consequences and long-term impact. It pervaded my psyche, remodeled my feelings and attitudes toward myself, and distorted my interactions with others and my relationship with the world.

When failure infiltrated my defenses, I pushed through it at first, as if it were a mild infection. I fought it off with hard work, ingrained optimism and self-assurances I was taught that kicked in like emotional auto-immunity— "Your luck can change in a second!" "Success is around the corner, in the next call, the next contact!" and "Just keep your chin up and keep believing."

But failure spread inside me and gradually took hold, making me violent and irascible. It raised the volume of my voice and gave it a shrill timbre. Did the others hear the ambient sound of failure, the rataplan filling the air like a savage drumbeat? Did they sense the pressure I was under?

Failure was the reaper, always a moment away from flaring up, yet otherwise working quietly with methodical precision. It discharged from its invasive cells a stream of bitterness, disinterest, anxiety and self-doubt that eroded ambition and poisoned desire. It prompted me to ask one question repeatedly, "Why am I doing this? Where does this lead?"

For weeks, months, and then years, failure migrated to every precinct of my brain. I wanted to believe it was a passing illness, a temporary setback, but eventually I had to acknowledge that my life was fast becoming a full-blown fiasco. It might be chronic and I had no clue what to do about it or how to seek help for it—if such help existed.

Intermittent losses of energy, heartsickness and disgust—with myself and with every aspect of my life—were some salient symptoms I endured. I cursed the ineffectuality of my endeavors and despised my poverty, evinced by the splintered window frames, the plastic floors and the vermin in my apartment. Even the panoramic window view of the city annoyed me.

I also felt revulsion for everyone with whom I came in contact— especially with anyone who made my life more difficult by crossing or rejecting me. Their reasons no longer mattered. All that counted was this disease that permeated and transfigured my life.

I did not wish to get to the bottom of failure, to learn why it happened. In my mind it was idiopathic, a blunt instrument of nature that lacked the appeal of a mystery. I became fatalistic. Though I felt stale, I did not wish to try something new. I was ossifying, desiccating and shriveling.

Finally, when failure was suffocating me in my monomaniacal pursuit of success, I backed off to try to save myself. I was resolved not to let failure be my fate. But that wasn't enough. Failure wasn't going anywhere. It would stay in me like any effective parasite—to consume me and keep me alive.

Failure: Trauma and Taboo

Failure is a taboo no one wishes to confront or discuss because it is a period, rather than a comma, in one's life. I tried to hide my failure from others, but what good was it to dissemble when I couldn't hide it from myself? One symptom I experienced was a profound humiliation that precluded me from making eye contact. I believed my inadequacy was palpable and conspicuous, discoloring me like jaundice.

There were remissions when I forgot my failure. I tried to make the most of these episodes of light by losing myself in the noise and clutter of the world. But the reproachful looks people gave me reinforced my abjection. The pity in their eyes and the disdain in their sardonic thin smiles scalded me. Their faces told me that I was a loser who made it possible for them to win. I could see them glancing away as I approached.

They must have felt sorry for me, that someone had to suffer so, yet they probably also feared the outcome they saw in me. They might have believed I could infect them if they looked too long or came too close to me. In their minds, I was an example of what bad ends may come to a good thing, a beautiful dream, a valiant effort.

At times these passersby seemed to feel responsibility for my state. Was there something they could do? But as they formulated the thought, they shuddered, passed briskly and saved themselves the trouble of answering their own question. They must have wished above all to be protected from the message my existence delivered to their own.

For a second they feared, or *knew*, my fate was a possibility for them but they lowered the shutters, closed the gates and chanted the mantra that success was their destiny. They had been warned that people brought failure on themselves because they were stupid, evil, undisciplined or masochistic.

I did not blame them for their preconceptions. They were no different than I had been. They viewed failure as living suicide, a ghastly fate. The individual who had been defeated wore his failure on his face like a stark tattoo. He was taboo: if you looked at, spoke to, or listened to him, his failure could infect and defile you.

I belonged to the lowest caste, like a pariah who handled corpses. One did not dare to interact with me because my defilement was communicable by contact, following the law of imitative magic. Yet, those who still trudged toward success glanced at me—I was irresistible to their sparks of doubt. They surmised from the poignancy in my face and manner that I was not a *bad* person. They believed I did not deserve to suffer.

But sympathy was dangerous, too. It might induce one to question the meaning of failure, doubt its justice or even lose one's dread of it. Learning a failed person's story might suggest that failure could happen to you, as well. It might cause you to admire the failed one's fortitude and recognize that under its demonic cloak, failure was a servant of life's randomness.

This was how failure took hold and even assumed a heroic character. It was safer to banish failure from one's thoughts and stay distant from anyone who made you think of it.

Coexisting with Failure

Failure suggests finality, yet it is chronic, not terminal. While it is possible to learn from failure and to live with it, it's not something I ever could "get over." However, I learned to manage it. As with all life events, I processed and converted failure into knowledge and memory. I put my critical mind to work, dissecting and classifying failure, dividing its causes from its effects. I compartmentalized and sealed off failure by linking it to specifics. In so doing I spared the rest of my life.

One therapeutic measure I took was to expunge "failure" from my vocabulary and replace it with the phrase, "haven't succeeded *yet*," which was renewable until my life was over. I also had the healing insight or self-serving delusion (they can seem interchangeable) that failure was not personal, but universal—experienced by all people. I conjectured that it might be integral to life, like senescence and death, as a foreshadowing of those dread events. To fail in one's purpose became a metaphor for biological failure. Mortality was the original lost cause; failure was how one prepared for it.

In the end, I had a simple choice—to dwell on failure or to be truly alive. After analyzing and rationalizing failure, I shrank it to a small and finite size and tried to wish it out of existence. But my conscious will could not destroy failure, so I found a place for it in a drawer in the back of my mind. I hoped that if I left it there, I'd forget about it and it would dwindle to nothing.

But failure didn't shrivel and die. It was like Osiris, slaughtered and butchered, with a beating heart and hidden in the darkness to which I relegated it, ready to be restored. Like all monsters, it indifferently waits until I am driven to look for it, think of it or speak its name.

One day, when I am tired and forlorn and lack the energy or spirit to do more than take stock of the jumble of projects I've attempted, the efforts I've made and the time I've wasted, I will think of failure and it will rush upon me.

Though I have spent so much time in the company of failure, contemplating and enduring its manifold effects, I hope I'll be prepared to stare it down and be free of it when we reunite for the last time.

PREGNANT EXHIBITIONIST

I once experienced a disconcerting conundrum of modern living for which I was unprepared. I worked with a woman art director who had red hair and the lissome, voluptuous form Chaucer described in *The Miller's Tale* as "graceful and slender as a weasel." My colleague was married and at some point she became pregnant. As her fetus grew inside her, her attire got tighter and more revealing. I wondered why a wife and mother-to-be wished to call attention to her body in a business setting, when such attention might seem perverse.

I knew the sensuous, pregnant art director's attire was my problem, not hers. She was entitled to wear what she wanted and I had no right to question or object to it. But the fact that I noticed her style and was provoked by it compelled me to seek answers and resolve my conflict.

I believed I was protected from such perturbations. Biology and culture were designed to inure men to the sexuality of pregnant women and to provide deterrents. For one, certain side effects of pregnancy, including nausea, fatigue, weight gain and unease, often made women feel less sexual and less attractive and were sex-repellents to men. But if this were true, the art director's sex repellent wasn't working hard enough on me.

Voluminous maternity clothes also generally did their part to hide (as behind a curtain) the fetus inside. Such apparel typically made women seem asexual.

However, the strongest bulwark against the allure of a pregnant woman was the cultural dichotomy between the Madonna and the whore—the Madonna unapproachable and irreproachable—that made mothers-to-be off-limits to men other than the father. This cultural distinction correlated with the biological purpose of sexual allure. Since attraction served the mating instinct, nothing said, "Taken!" like a pregnant abdomen.

But this fashion-forward pregnant art director outflanked my emotional barriers and I was embarrassed by her effect on me.

I felt like a freak of nature, though I was not the first or the most prominent one. Livia was seven months pregnant when a love-smitten Augustus Caesar compelled her to divorce her husband and marry him. After she gave birth, Romans gossiped that the emperor was surely a god to have hurried gestation so dramatically.

I was so agitated by my unprofessional distraction that I discussed it with a friend, who was training to be a life coach. Since he had already tested some of his theories on me, he took my bait and provided two interpretations for my pregnant colleague's fashion choices and my reaction to them.

"Your colleague is the screen on which all things internal are projected," my friend the life coach explained.

This explanation required an explanation, which the apprentice life coach was keen to provide.

"You mentioned that she's attractive," he remarked. "She has always been aware of her sexuality and her pregnancy makes her more so. She projects the purposes and effects of her sexuality writ large on every amplified curve of her pregnant body and it touches your deepest longings. Her pregnancy calls out to your masculinity, your drive to procreate."

I was impressed by this insight, yet it did not slake my thirst for knowledge.

"So what's your second theory?" I asked.

He paused. In the afterglow of his bravura analysis, my friend believed he had done all that was required to convince me—and he forgot his alternate interpretation.

"The second reason for your discomfort is biochemical," he resumed. "Like solar winds thrust outward into the solar system by a hyperactive sun, your captivating colleague may be emanating massive amounts of bioelectric hormones in all directions. Pregnant women are hormone factories. Since you are an extremely sensitive male, your dish is being flooded with signals and stimuli. It's no secret that many women report surges in sexuality during the first six months of pregnancy."

Ironically, I was writing intensively on hormone replacement therapy at the time, so I thought I knew a bit about these potent molecules and the mischief they could make. Clearly, my pregnant colleague's hormones and mine were running amok, but this situation went beyond that.

"That is a brilliant insight," I told my friend the life coach. "Really first-rate. I understand the biological, psychological and hormonal stimuli for her behavior. She's always been attractive. It's hard-wired in her personality. In her mind and heart she remains the same woman, only more so, and she can't stop. That makes sense—*for her*. But why am I going through this? I shouldn't care what she wears and how she looks. And I shouldn't make spurious distinctions between a regular woman and a pregnant one. *But I do*. And it's killing me. I have intense cognitive dissonance with her when I want to be harmonious and blasé."

My friend softly chuckled on the other end of the line. He was assuming a counseling demeanor—wise, tolerant and superior. Meanwhile, I felt pathetic and ridiculous, like a mental guinea pig being poked and probed by his analytical mind. Yet I earnestly hoped something he said would free me.

"There is a third factor to your unease," he said portentously, as if this were the ultimate, last resort, no-holds-barred interpretation reserved for the most dire cases. "We're always having feelings about people around us. It's so normal that we rarely admit them to ourselves. You may have felt something for your art director colleague, though you have a strictly professional relationship and lead separate lives. Now bear with me. This is the crazy part.

"You've always *known* she was married and you respected her status. At the same time, you saw her everyday and couldn't help unconsciously picturing yourself with her. But now that she's pregnant, her intimate life slaps your unconscious fantasies in the face. Her rounded belly, her engorged nipples, everything about her body is incredibly full and real and you realize what you've imagined about her is only fantasy. In short, her pregnancy makes you jealous."

"Oh no!" I clutched my face and covered my eyes in response to his nuclear interpretation. "I've been mentally unfaithful with a pregnant woman. Now I know how Oedipus felt."

"He had sex with his mother. You're only lusting for a pregnant woman. There's a difference," the life coach intern remarked to assuage my guilt. "Here's what you can do. Acknowledge your attraction and accept your feelings without judging them. They're honest and pure. Relax and appreciate the wonders your eyes behold. Capture all the *Eros* that pours from your hormone-engorged colleague and give it later to your wife."

"You're advising me to be aroused by my pregnant co-worker and then have sex with my wife?"

He paused. "That's the plan."

"No!" I protested. "That can't be right."

I believed my unofficial life coach had over-diagnosed my agitation and prescribed the wrong treatment.

Yes, I was perplexed and distressed by my pregnant colleague's coupling of two female images—the temptress and the mother. But I wondered if my reaction to her provocative style was unnatural and amiss. Was I a prude, hard-wired to see women as mothers, virgins or whores, or justifiably confused by the fusion of motherhood and sexuality when the pregnant art director showed up in a partly unbuttoned, form-fitting body suit that revealed the swell of her bosom and accentuated every other distended curve of her life-giving physique? Pregnancy was so intimate, yet she bared it to the world.

This was a new cultural twist in the normal biological schema.

I had hitherto viewed pregnant women as asexual for a good reason. Pregnancy announced that a woman's womb was taken, removing a powerful male sexual stimulus. And once a woman was pregnant, her commitment was to her child. She lost the seductress mask and became the nurturing protector. Whether a woman emitted these signals or whether they were projected upon her was unclear. Yet this transformation was represented in the oxymoron of the 'virgin mother', a concept embedded in human culture. A mother traded in her eroticism for the power of creating new life.

The ancients believed this power could be both nurturing and harsh. Cybele, the goddess of fertility, was the original "castrating bitch" whose priests offered up their genitals to her flame of sacrifice. Cybele was the embodiment of male fears about mothers. It distilled in myth the fact that childbirth separated women from men, made them more powerful and less compliant with men's wishes.

Of course, men were complicit in the concept of the sexless, demanding mother. The mother imago and the temptress were both figments of the male psyche. Men respected and feared the power of motherhood. To neutralize and manage it, men confined and consecrated motherhood within the walls of the home and the domestic role we wished mothers to play—the clean, caring, sexless fulfiller of basic needs.

We had eons of practice doing this.

Hera, the goddess of marriage and birth and Zeus's wife, was never depicted as sexual, but as the perpetual tormentor of her philandering husband and his concubines. Hera's severity was justified by her purpose—to preserve the sanctity of the family. Meanwhile, the Virgin Mary portrayed the giving and forgiving side of the asexual mother; to view her in sexual terms would be self-defeating, since sexuality would raise concerns and demands, rather than give comfort.

Regardless of how much of my attitude toward pregnant women was my invented hang-up or one received by a patriarchal culture, I wished for my colleague and all pregnant women to uphold my sanctimonious preconceptions. I could not accept that a woman could be pregnant and provocative, flaunting her body and daring men to admire it. I was exposed as a surreptitious sexist, who supported equality, while wishing to regulate how women expressed their sexuality.

This was a significant breakthrough in self-awareness, but I was unable to act on it. My crisis over the sexy, pregnant colleague did not resolve itself because larger events supervened. The agency lost accounts, my pregnant colleague went on maternity leave and I moved on to another job. I never saw her again but the story didn't end there.

It would resurface years later. During that interval, a cultural taboo had apparently fallen between women and pregnancy. Meanwhile my dichotomous conception of women and the image women had of themselves had also evolved. The female coin with Mother Mary as heads and Aphrodite as tails was no longer in circulation.

Encountering a woman's uninhibited fashion statement during pregnancy had evidently modified my perspective. I now understood that a woman's choice encompassed not only her decision to be pregnant but also how she wished to show her body to the world.

I was in a status meeting with several women, three of whom were in the third term of their pregnancies. To my surprise, they wore normal office attire—pants, form-fitting tops and sweaters—and looked as natural in their woolens, knits and tweeds as they were with the fetuses inside them. They had struck a balance between concealment and self-exposure.

Even on TV, which confirms social norms, a female anchorwoman in a snug mini-dress that embraced every swell of her pregnant body presented the day's news in a crisp, professional manner, which suggested that her wardrobe was not intended to invite undue attention but to dismiss it. The duality of mother and slut was never a woman's paradigm and this mother-to-be did not feel obliged to conform to it.

A pregnant woman no longer wears an asterisk. Childbearing is a fact for which she does not hide or apologize. She dresses as she likes and doesn't care what others think. Her only statement is that she has not renounced her style, even as her body changes. She announces to anyone who cares to listen, "My body is different for now but I'm the same person I was before. Treat me that way."

THE POWER OF PRAYER

I was in Riverdale, New York, a cozy, middle class enclave beyond the subways, on a bluff between the Hudson River and the roiling city that lowers its shoulders to the sea. On a busy corner in front of a Starbucks, a team of Lubavitcher Jewish teenagers were on the prowl for Jewish souls, approaching every male passerby with the question, "Are you Jewish?"

If the distracted and unsuspecting soul answered in the affirmative, the Hasidic teenagers asked a follow up, "Did you make *tefillin* today?"

If the man responded that he had not "made tefillin" that day the young Lubavitcher evangelists pleaded with the unobservant Jew to spare 30 seconds to learn how to use *tefillin*.

Tefillin are prayer phylacteries, two black cubes with straps attached to them. The black boxes contain strips of paper printed with lines of Jewish scripture. Every Jewish man over the age of 13 is required by the Torah to wear *tefillin* once a day as a sign of devotion.

"And you shall bind them for a sign upon your hand, and they shall be for ornaments between your eyes" it says in Deuteronomy 6:8. One of the *tefillin* boxes is placed on the forehead and held there by a leather headband with straps trailing down the back. The second cube fits on the bicep, close to the heart. The straps of the arm *tefillin* are wound seven times around the arm and three times around a middle finger.

I descried the young Hasids milling on the corner as I parked halfway up the block and resolved to avoid the young neighborhood missionaries. I don't object to their mission to promote religious observance and ethnic pride with Jews; to the contrary, I like their large mobile menorahs on Hanukkah and their *lulavs* and *esrogs* at Sukkot. I knew they were out that afternoon to tout Shavuot—the holiday commemorating when Moses delivered the Torah to the Israelites—momentous, mythic stuff—but I had to buy shaving cream and a cup of coffee before returning to my neighborhood to look for parking.

When I approached the corner I veered as far as possible from the

Lubavitcher youths and bee-lined for the drug store. They didn't seem to notice me and I thought that they might not have identified me as a Jew. But after I made my pharmacy purchase and headed to the Starbucks, they detected me.

"Sir, are you Jewish?"

"Yes."

"Did you do *tefillin* today?"

"No."

I might have lied that I wasn't Jewish or that I had used *tefillin* that morning, but I couldn't. I'm not observant but I am superstitious. I cannot lie about matters of faith to ardent believers because to do so demeans what they hold dearest, the meaning of their lives.

"Can you spare 30 seconds learning how to do *tefillin*?" the leader repeated.

"I have *tefillin*. I know how to use them. But I won't use them."

"Sir, if you do it once, it will be a *mitzvah*. Please, it won't take more than 30 seconds."

As I approached the coffee shop, I tried to be firmly agnostic, yet courteous to the young zealots who made such a humble if misguided request. I was resistant but not hostile to their cause. I wasn't buying what they were selling but I didn't want to be rude or hurt their feelings.

"I appreciate what you're doing," I said so they wouldn't feel like rejects and failures. I opened the door of the café. "I'm just not interested."

With that declaration of principled agnosticism and tolerance I entered the Starbucks, believing I had amicably settled the matter. Surely, the young Hasids would leave me alone and we would diverge in peace.

As I waited for a batch of coffee to be brewed, I reflected on my attitudes and feelings toward *tefillin* and religious faith in general.

I did not lie to the Hasidic youths. I still owned the *tefillin* I received at my *bar mitzvah*. The last time I'd used them was when I was thirteen. For a month of summer mornings I used the phylacteries at home until I lost interest in my lonely ritual and forgot about them.

I commended the idealism and good will of these young men, even if I did not agree with their views. I am not averse to prayer. To the contrary, I pray every day—but I recite my own prayer, one I created, committed to memory and revised over the years. This little prayer of mine is no supplication to an omnipotent deity. Nor do I expect my modest entreaties to impact a vast universe. Why then do I pray? Because it comforts me to believe I'm doing something when I'm not, that I can control my life and protect the lives of others I love when it's unclear that I can.

When I emerged from the coffee shop ten minutes later, the same tenacious missionaries in white shirttails and dark suits awaited me. "Sir! Sir! Can we show you how to use *tefillin*?"

Some coffee splashed out of my cup and burned my fingers. I thought I'd be better off confronting them than making a break for my car although the meter had expired. I had to handle them with diplomatic speed.

"Please, I have to get to my car," I insisted nervously as I turned the corner and accelerated down the street. "I don't want a parking ticket."

"We can go with you to your car and show you the *tefillin* there," the lead evangelist insisted as he tagged along. "It will only take 30 seconds."

The young orthodox soul seekers tagged after me and it was clear that I wasn't going to shake them with fast walking, balking and affable objections. When we arrived at my car, I conceded. "Okay, I'll do the *tefillin*. But first I'll put away my coffee or it's going to scald me."

"Great!" the lead evangelist replied. Then to reward my compliance, he added, "It'll be over in no time. We'll just do the head *tefillin*."

I knew he was making a false promise. Arm *tefillin* always go first. I also knew that observant Jews are never satisfied with half measures in ritual and faith.

Now three *Lubavitcher* boys hovered around me in the street next to my car. The eager leader placed one black cube on my forearm next to my heart and recited a prayer specific to *tefillin*, before wrapping the straps seven times around my arm and three times around my finger. He said the *Shema* and had me repeat it. I stood in the middle of the street, wearing phylacteries, feeling conspicuous, incongruous and, given my agnostic lack of belief, ridiculous.

After the demonstration, the leader, who introduced himself as Menachem, unwound the *tefillin* straps from my arm and said, "You've done a great thing, sir. The world is a better place. Do you feel happy?"

He nodded effusively with wide eyes, expecting me, coaxing me, to confirm that a magical transformation had taken place in me.

"I'm happy because *you're* happy," I replied.

This Zen-style boomerang surprised the boys. How could I be happy for them when I was the one receiving the gift of a lifetime? They thought I must have it wrong—but they *were* happy. They came for this reason and they were flushed and brimming with success at a mission fulfilled. As they grinned and nodded and shifted from one foot to the other, they looked like a sports team that had scored a goal and won a game.

It is not a tortured association. Religion has often been associated with conquest in language and in deed. Who could ignore all the smiting in the Bible, the threats, the curses and the wars against one's enemies?

I mused on the Crusades, the Conquistadors' conquest and conversion of the Aztecs and the Incas, and the Muslim forays across Asia, Africa and Spain—all to the soundtrack of hymns and chants that God is good.

These lanky yeshiva boys were unlikely crusaders—or missionaries, for that matter. I could not imagine them fulminating against infidels and putting pagans to the sword. Yet they were just as zealous in their faith as their truculent historical counterparts and equally hell-bent on converting secular Jews to the word of God and the 613 commandments of the Torah.

After we introduced ourselves and shook hands as a congenial afterthought, the young *Hasids* flocked to their corner to seek one more Jewish man for a *tefillin* lesson. Or, having done enough righteous deeds for the time being, they were off to *shul* for the Shabbos service.

I meanwhile drove off to spend Friday night in my secular home. Nothing had changed, yet the young Jewish zealots were ecstatic at their transitory triumph. Inducing me to perform a religious act was a blessing for them. The good feeling rubbed off on me, as well, because by accepting a gift and cooperating for a moment, I gave a sense of accomplishment and cheer to others at no harm to myself.

HUMILITY AND HUMILIATION

Arrogance is an obnoxious quality, and a dangerous one, since it is a predicate for many other personal failings and general calamities. Arrogance can manipulate, betray and destroy, yet false humility is worse. While conceit can amplify a weak voice, mask a lack of integrity and strength, and shield against self-doubt, false humility is often egotism in disguise and does significant damage before it can be detected.

Why do I dwell on arrogance and false humility? Because I have been accused of the former and am incapable of the latter. Yet there is a third alternative—genuine humility—which aggrieves me most of all. My life has been dogged by a lack of humility or by my inability to fake the attitude. I have often been pilloried for reveling in the few things I do well and exulting unabashedly in every small victory I achieve.

For years I had no idea that I lacked humility or that it was a useful tool to have. I believed it was enough to "be myself" and to impress others that I was capable and employable. My experience confirmed that the world was inflated like a beach ball with self-promotion and self-importance. In this context, I did not fit in perfectly but well enough.

Fortunately, people who cared about me said I had a humility deficit and urged me to seek help. I consulted with humility experts—a professional athlete, an actor and a brain surgeon—admittedly not the most humble people, themselves. Yet they all pointed out that humility correlated with insight, while its absence signified a lack of self-awareness.

With no intuitive grasp for the concept of humility, I tried to approach it analytically from the outside. What was this elusive property I lacked and where did it originate? However, seeking the right words for a concept I couldn't decode was like putting clothes on an entity without knowing its shape, height and weight. I had to guess at humility by knowing what it *wasn't*.

No one ever mistook me for humble but I was often called arrogant. Now arrogance was a quality I comprehended though I did not believe it pertained to me. Yes, I had confidence but how could I strive or survive without it? My self-assurance was not based on delusions of grandeur but on special attributes cultivated over time. Yet, teachers, supervisors and peers often suggested that my self-belief was a character flaw.

Over time, their reproof overcame my petulant resistance. I saw humility as a better way to go than conceit and I tried to adopt it. Yet, while the practical value of cultivating humility was now apparent to me, I was unable to grasp it and I made little progress.

No one was available to explain humility to me. Either people didn't know what it was or it was abstruse information possessed by a select few. I might have sought occupational therapy to impart humble skills if I knew where to find it but no one seemed to specialize in this recondite practice. Paragons of humility were cited for my emulation. I watched their videos but the tokens and gestures of humility they demonstrated might as well have been the secret signs of a fraternity of chimpanzees for all the meaning I derived from them.

What is humility, after all? Like talent, intellect and charm, it is a puzzle, internal and intangible, intuited rather than perceived—and highly subjective. For some, it is the deliberate self-abasement of the princess who kissed lepers' lesions for the love of God. Or it is the self-acknowledged subordination of a servant to a master. Is it poor self-esteem or the acknowledgement of failure, the ultimate self-control or unconditional surrender? I received no answers. The prevailing attitude seemed to be that of the immortal jazzman who was asked to define "swing." "If you have to ask," he said, "you'll never know."

Maybe I had learned humility without knowing it from those who rejected me and made me suffer failure and doubt. If this was their goal, or an unintended consequence of their cruelty, I should have thanked them. Perhaps I was humble now by default, though the only emotions I was conscious of feeling were rage and confusion. Regardless of how many humility lessons I had received, I still believed I deserved honor and success. On the other hand, those who brought me down may not have been imparting humility. What I obtained from them was different—

humiliation, which passes for humility but is as different from it as a mushroom is from a toadstool. In fact, humiliation might have been my obstacle to humility.

Despite my inability to express humility, I persisted in trying to acquire it. I did not wish to improve my character but to bring myself peace and contentment. Arrogance was my protective armor but it did not produce happiness. It was an imaginary friend, a simulated support, a counterfeit wealth, a private fame, a loss masquerading as success. Arrogance was a fine wardrobe, while humility was simple nudity, self-effacing but unashamed.

Humility eluded me even as I continued to strive for it. It was like an exotic paradisiac place where I had never been but where I believed happiness resided. I convinced myself that having humility might improve my life by making me more likable. It presented itself to my imagination as an exalted membership to an elite society, the final flourish in a profile. People would say, "He's so talented and successful—and so humble."

But humility was not without risk. It meant submitting to the other, and I wasn't sure who or what this other was. So I tried to be humble everywhere and on all occasions. I tried to be deferential and reserved, passive and compliant, but who witnessed and approved of my spiritual contortions? Who was there to decide if I was humble or not? As much as I wanted to feel it, I couldn't seem to cross over to humility.

Still I persevered. I refused to grimace because this might suggest anger and discontent, that I felt I deserved more and better—which was the antithesis of humility. I cultivated an obsequious demeanor that would make anyone whose eyes met mine feel superior to me. I hoped that once I refined this persona, people would appreciate my humility and reward me for it—though I had no idea what this compensation would be.

I relied on observation and mimesis to simulate humility. I walked with a bowed head and smiled benignly for no reason. I cultivated a stoop and a shuffle and affected humility as if it were a neurological disease. But I was all caricature, not character. I hoped my mannerisms would work from the outside in but I only parodied humility.

My bad acting never worked because nothing rings as false as false humility. Instead of approval, people treated me with a disgust as thinly masked as I was; they no longer viewed me as an arrogant individual they disliked, but as a snarky fake whom they were entitled to despise.

Despite my contrivances, I was as clueless about humility as I had been before I started. "Why can't I be humble?" I cried. "It makes no sense. I am downtrodden, unfulfilled and miserable, yet I can't be humble!" It was distressing. I had compromised my dignity and suppressed my personality for naught—since I was no more liked and respected than before. Humility was like a bad hair transplant—it did not take root. I needed a new approach.

I sought inspiration and instruction but the world dispatched weird messages about humility. For instance, it was attributed to rich and famous people who exuded self-importance. This oxymoron perplexed and infuriated me because it undermined logic and experience. What sense did it make for individuals to be humble when they had worked single-mindedly for importance? It seemed like a trick to bestow an unexpected virtue on someone who clearly lacked it. Conversely, humility might be a luxury, an honor or a gift for someone who had everything. Was humility egotism's crown?

Yes! This, I discovered, was the secret of humility. It was a quality that paired best with success, since it would only be conspicuous in a person in whom it was unexpected. Surprise was its appeal. It was entertaining to hear a rich man downplay his acumen, an artist to rank his dumb luck above his genius, an athlete to credit God, hard work and teammates for his superstardom. It was rich to hear these celebrities talk about themselves in such incredible ways.

However the incongruous humility of pompous people provided insight. I realized that humility was beyond my reach for two reasons. The external cause was that humility was too exalted for my status. How could I be humble when I was abject? No one gets credit for stating the obvious, and the troll who proclaims his lowly stature takes his place in universal scorn. His humility is facile when the rule of virtue is that it must be hard.

The internal reason for my humility deficit was harder to accept. Humility and humiliation both trim the ego but they cannot be more different from one another. Humility is voluntary, what a person does, while humiliation is involuntary, what is done to him. The same distinction can be made between discipline and deprivation. Humility is to deny one's self-approval, while humiliation is to be denied the respect of others. Because I was tainted by humiliation, I was disqualified from being humble.

Humility is the face of grace, which few have and others can only behold. It is like being saved—you know it when it happens, but you can't describe it. It is rooted in a deep security and is predicated on abundance. The one who is praised for humility exudes good fortune but never mentions it. He bears it lightly by pretending it doesn't exist. For this reason, he does not bear the burden of defending it, losing it or revealing how he gained it.

Humility may also be an act. Celebrities do not need to boast because publicists do it for them. Such modesty is tantamount to not carrying a driver's license when you have a chauffeur. It is both a privilege and smart public relations not to peddle oneself.

After research and reflection, I realized I could never be humble. I wanted to possess this glittering attribute but it was as futile as learning to be smart or beautiful. I would have to survive without it.

The path of humility was barred to me because humiliation had brought me low and stood before the gate toward which I crawled. Humility and humiliation are rival siblings that cannot coexist in one individual. They are chimeric emotions, apparently close, yet radically different, and constantly at odds. I console myself that humility is not solely the special virtue of a saint but a commodity affluent pride can buy. A humiliated soul like mine may not withstand humility because if I bow, I may break.

TIME IS NOT MONEY

One bane of American life is the false claim that time is money. Derived from the Protestant work ethic, the ideological axis of America, the time/money equivalence has been warped into one more source of frustration (as if we needed another) for millions who subscribe to it.

When Ben Franklin declared, "If you love life then value time, for time is the stuff life is made of," he was not exhorting anyone to run red lights, push people from behind or cut them off in mid-sentence because they might be depriving us of precious seconds with their bafflegab. He was only admonishing us to make the most of the time we have.

Granted, the time we are *given* is always less than what we need or deserve. It is only what circumstance allows. I accept this agonizing fact without defiance or resentment in order to function with a modicum of happiness and calm. Yet I cannot abide the time/money formula because it is a false construct that fails to acknowledge the incalculable uncertainty of existence. Equating money and time establishes an unrealistic expectation that never fails to disappoint us.

I am so involved in time that I imagine it is involved with me. It isn't. Time is impervious to my purposes and outcomes. It knows and cares nothing about winning, losing, saving and spending. I try to control time by translating it into financial terms and other metaphors of value but it is not contained in vaults or chips and it cannot be bartered.

Indeed, time is so precious that I wish it were money because I believe I can understand and control money. But my good uses of time may in the long run be viewed as wasteful, depending on their outcomes. How many false starts and bad endings now fill my file cabinets and closets and turn my living space into a graveyard of broken promises and withered dreams?

The fault lies in my notion of time. I have believed it is a useful thing. But time is not productive. It simply is. It flows by, through and around me. It is that clear, fluid stuff that absorbs my hopes, desires and ambitions, but only rarely abets them.

Even when I stick to a tight schedule, I save time in one place only to lose it in another. After hoarding minutes, I dissipate a year of hours in waiting rooms, courtrooms, laundromats, government facilities or workplaces that go out of business. When I receive 24 hours for a national holiday, I spend most of it sleeping, standing in a checkout line and sitting in traffic with others who also helplessly hemorrhage time.

Converting time into money is modern alchemy. It presumes that time is fungible, redeemable for cash. Yet for time to be saved and well spent, one would need a universal standard by which every task and activity would be assigned a specific duration. Completing a task in less than the predetermined time would signify a savings, exceeding it would count as a waste, and filling it would amount to breaking even.

However time is never saved. Anyone who has done anything or gone anywhere by any means for any reason knows the futility of trying to predict how much time it will take to accomplish even modest objectives. Wasting time seems to be what time was meant for, just as food is meant to be eaten and air to be breathed.

Time as a measure of efficiency and profit might be sensible if all people and their time were equal—which is not the case. Time is divided in 24 zones and by many more degrees of status. Anyone who has worked long hours at menial tasks or stood in a queue while VIPs were whisked into a venue can vouch for this disparity. When I was a new salesman, a prospective local client granted me a meeting at 2PM and made me wait until 2:30 while he lunched and played checkers with a friend. He was letting me know we could do business only after I conceded that his time was worth more than mine.

Time is an abstraction that is adapted to our economic and social hierarchy. It measures status because it has been quantified and monetized in our market-driven world, the values of which it reinforces and reflects.

The ongoing conflict over the minimum wage confirms that time is most unequal in determining the value of work and its reward. The social and economic status of an individual and his access to capital determine what his time is worth. For some, a one-minute phone call may yield a million dollars, more than others working 60,000 hours in their lifetimes will ever come close to earning.

Ever since my first afterschool job, I have been plugged into the time/money equation—all the way from pocket change to the minimum wage to driving a cab with a meter running to earning a hundred dollars per hour. Yet the value of my time never enhanced my personal value. To the contrary, when my time was worth most to others, I was most abused. I earned more in advertising than in other occupations because my employers established a high hourly rate for my time, which they billed to their clients. Clients were aware of this arrangement and they might have been expected to spend my time with greater thrift, but they were as demanding as children and misused my overpriced commodity.

Regardless of how hard I worked to expedite my projects during business hours, clients inevitably called at day's end to make rash changes that generated more work and billable hours. They insisted on seeing what they wanted first thing in the morning, which burned my time and their money through the night. The agency was happy with this, so when I protested that I wished to go home at normal hours to see my family, they rebuked me, "Why do you complain? We pay you for your time."

Time is as promiscuous as money. We receive it, use it and everything we do requires it. But time is not money. We can know in a flash the amount in a bank account but we're never sure how much time we have. Money can belong to us but time never does. It comes between us and exceeds our grasp. We try to appropriate it but it is a resource under perpetual negotiation—determined by allies and adversaries, projects and obligations. From the moment we're born, our time is never our own.

The "time-share" may be a discredited product but it articulates a basic truth—time *is* shared. When we mark off time like a plot of land and try to guard it against the abuse or disregard of others, we're doomed to fail because time is not only measured by sand—it *is* sand, shifting in size and location. I plan my project but whether I spend a day or a year to fulfill it depends on others. Supervisors, colleagues, contractors—even the weather—determine the quality of my time.

Time=money is a formula for social disaster. It incites us to fight, cheat and hate one another out of anxiety and impatience spurred by an impossible demand. Colleagues, commuters and vendors stand between me and my time. The car in front steals a minute. The crossing pedestrian takes another. Automated voices swallow my day in option menus. I count on technology to save time, but when technology fails, it gushes hours and days like a ruptured pipeline. It feels so futile. Why do we do this to each other? Why do we waste one another's time when time is all we have?

Time can be counted but never counted on. Yet when I've had the option of time or money I've chosen time because it yields the most generous rate of return. Time permits me to collect my thoughts and put them in order. With time, the best of me emerges.

Even so, I've paid a price for putting time before money. Employers declined my services when I denied them every nanosecond of my life, forcing me to spend weeks and months seeking other jobs. Bosses wanted my help but what they coveted most was my time.

Some years ago, my tumultuous relationship with time boiled to a crisis. I craved it, struggled with it, fought for it, was tortured by and possessed by it. A meter was perpetually running in my head. The dial spun rapidly and I could never stop it, slow it down or catch up with it. Something had to change. Time wasn't going to change, so it had to be me.

I forced myself to sit quietly in a dark room and let time unwind in my head. In the stillness, I realized that time was only something I used. I valued it to the extent that I filled it. Only what I did mattered, not the time in which I did it. Time was an empty expanse.

Then I asked myself what it might be like to experience time as something independent of its utility. I tried to visualize it but nothing came to me until I returned to a distant memory. I was 20 years old, traveling in Europe with a friend. On our way to Amsterdam, the car broke down in a rural area of Belgium. We walked to the nearest farm where a kindly woman let us call a repair shop.

As we waited for the mechanic, the woman painstakingly peeled and cut carrots and spilled the orange dices into a bowl. She worked in slow and methodical silence. As I watched her, I was acutely aware of time passing, though she was impervious to it. Then I slipped into a conscious but trancelike state when time apparently stopped and pulled up a chair at the kitchen table next to me to watch the woman and her diced carrots. Time was in the room and it wasn't doing a thing.

Maybe Ben Franklin was only partially right. Time is not to be only valued and used. If we love life, we should *experience* time, since time is not what life is made of—it *is* life.

This insight contradicted all that I had been taught. From an early age, teachers admonished me to budget my time, as if such a task were possible. As a child from a home embroiled in domestic violence, I knew then that time was subject to context and circumstance. I tried to dam and channel time but it always breached my levees and drowned my plans.

Agonizing to save a few minutes, I spent years paying for my haste. As I tried to outwit those who made a sport of spilling my time over muddy ground, they did what they could to outmaneuver me. The only way out of the trap was to uncouple time and money.

I lost countless hours obsessing over wasted time until I realized that it is squandered only if what I work at, wait for and strive after means more than who I am and what I have—this breath, this moment, this feeling, this thought. Time cannot be saved or increased, protected or manipulated— but it can be more fully experienced. It exists apart, yet if I feel and acknowledge its presence, it can move with and through me, but never against me.

FEAR OF GETTING PERSONAL

We may have taken the admonition "Don't take it personally" way too personally. In a world where "Don't go there" is a mantra, many of us are *shut-ins* when it comes to posing direct personal questions to people we know, in particular with regard to *sensitive* matters. We may be overly concerned that such inquiries will go tactlessly off-track and into the danger zones of private struggle and grief.

My wife once asked a woman she knew, whose son was in my daughter's class, how her younger son was doing. My wife had learned from another mother that this woman's younger son was stricken with schizophrenia, had been withdrawn from school and placed in a treatment facility, and she wished to reach out to her.

"Not very well," the mother answered my wife. "In fact, his situation is about as bad as it can be. But thank you for asking. Nobody ever does."

The mother's sincere response curled with irony. She thanked my wife for caring enough to raise an excruciating topic, for acknowledging the existence of her son, even in his debilitated condition, and for thus exposing herself vicariously to the situation. This must have been a rare enough gesture to raise comment. Apparently, this woman preferred having her family trauma addressed to having it buried in tactful omission.

Before this young boy was diagnosed, he had been a pupil at my daughter's school. When his psychological problems surfaced, he was withdrawn from his class. His former classmates must have remarked his absence, yet none of their parents, who interacted with his mother on a daily basis and knew about his tribulations, inquired about his whereabouts and welfare, or acknowledged that he had ever been enrolled with their children.

His illness had stricken him from their record, and by never mentioning him to his mother, they may have wished to remove from her any shibboleth she bore for his flawed existence. Maybe they believed that they were respecting her privacy, protecting her feelings—or their own—or simply minding their own business, which, admittedly, often seems the safest approach to a sensitive personal or family matter.

In our fastidious need to keep our lives simple and clean, we may believe that pain is the part of people's lives they wish to forget, conceal or have discreetly ignored. We view other people's problems as we would their trash, bad habits or bad taste—as generic and universal afflictions—and overlook them if they are out of our sight.

The studious effort to avoid direct contact with other people's pain is familiar behavior that we learn from an early age. It is the down-to-earth, day-to-day diplomacy that makes us refrain from the mention of a foul odor or a deformity. As children, we were adjured not to stare at or comment on other people's defects, regardless of how curious and enthralling they were. As adults, we raise this barrier of social refinement to exclude any item that does not fit in the "parental guidance" (PG) range. When we encounter an object or behavior that seems too private, intimate or shameful for us to witness, we demur and dismiss it as inappropriate.

Is this delicacy so deeply ingrained in us a renunciation or repression of our morbid attraction to others' troubles? That is a doubtful interpretation. If such graciousness existed, the news would not be a litany of natural and manmade catastrophes, fatalities, calamities and downfalls befalling ordinary people and celebrities.

We feast on others' misfortunes—from afar. Distance is the key factor in whether we relish or eschew a personal tragedy. Disaster on the news, notwithstanding how vast or gruesome it is, is never entirely real for us. It affects our imaginations because it is too remote for us to experience its palpable horror. We internalize remote gruesomeness as a therapeutic abstraction and intone the prayer, "There by the grace of God go I."

News is not alone in conveying human misery. Woes of neighbors and acquaintances appeal to our sensibilities when we obtain them from secondary sources. We love knowing about the setbacks that befall others, but we don't want to hear the victims tell us about their vicissitudes firsthand. We want their story from a third party in the form of gossip, which is misery trafficked and traded as social currency or entertainment.

One receives such illicit goods with an exciting tinge of transgression. Gossip is like the meat in a supermarket. It is a product removed from its source, from the pain of its origin. We consume other people's neatly packaged problems with alacrity because we are not compelled to acknowledge what the individual has suffered to produce it.

By contrast, when we hear the same dismal tale from the source we are compelled to take the pain seriously, to *take it in*. It necessitates that we accept their story as real and that we recognize the possibility of that tragedy as our own.

The wish to avoid direct contact with another person's pain may be pragmatic. It could be derived from the same mentality that authors the cursory exchange: "Hello, how are you, fine, how are you, thank you," or the shortened version, "Hey!" spoken in various tones from intimate to hail-fellow-well-met, depending on the degree of amiability the speaker wishes to convey. It is the "You've-got-your-troubles, I've got mine" attitude that asks no questions since one has no time or emotion to give.

Other peoples' problems might also distract us from our goals and responsibilities. Their tragedies could penetrate the defenses we need to survive, wounding our confidence with reasonable doubt about our fragility. Hearing their miseries firsthand might shake our security by putting us face to face with outcomes we dread for ourselves.

Listening to others' ordeals also makes us feel helpless. While we listen, we feel their pain. Yet we are at a loss as to what can we do to help them. Their hardship makes us feel vulnerable *and* useless—two attributes we will do anything to avoid.

Or perhaps we hesitate to ask a touchy question due to awkwardness. What can one reply to a death or devastating illness in a family? Any comment beyond a simple statement of sorrow and support sounds irrelevant and disrespectful.

However, the strongest motivator for avoiding getting personal is the most primitive one. We are afraid to touch, or be touched by, someone afflicted by disaster. Magical thinking seizes us: we believe misfortune is contagious and that our physical proximity will cause it to spread to us.

Contiguous magic, primitive cause and effect, re-emerges in our sophisticated minds as emotional hygiene. Any inquiry about another person's difficulties seems like a break in the skin. We believe their trouble will invade our lives. By avoiding others' debacles, we preclude them from infecting us. Our defect is not callousness, but empathy so intense that we internalize and *fear* others' miseries when we hear of them. One must be tough to be compassionate.

The fear of getting personal is personal to me. When I was growing up I often listened to others' problems on a regular basis. Troubled peers and even some adults identified me as someone to whom they could confide their painful secrets. I never understood why they selected me for this intimate role; perhaps I had a kind and thoughtful face or looked like I didn't have other friends to talk to or things to think about.

For a while, I didn't mind getting personal with others. Being a sounding board made me feel useful, even wanted in an odd way. As a teenager, it became one of my principal social interactions, though not the kind I truly wanted. People who discussed their intimate difficulties with me talked about nothing else. We never became fast friends because when it came to "getting personal," they were always giving and I was always receiving. While absorbing others' troubles gave me respite from my own, even this perquisite lost its luster. My problems were still waiting for me when I stopped listening to theirs and I realized that it would have been nice to have someone hear mine for a change.

As a consequence of this experience, I stopped getting personal with people and even grew averse to it. I felt guilty about my revulsion because I knew people needed help. At the same time, I wondered if listening to others' problems had genuine value. What was the point of asking and listening when there was little I could do to help? My concern for others seemed gratuitous. Their misfortunes weren't going away because we talked them over. Sunlight may be the best disinfectant but it rarely shines on the tormented heart.

I agonized over this dilemma and must have worn my internal conflict on my face as I sat on a bench in the park. A familiar stranger, a woman

106

who often fed the squirrels, said hello and we started to talk. At first, we chatted about the squirrels that pranced to the nuts she tossed on the sidewalk and the grass, sniffed them, handled them in their nervous paws and made off with their treasures.

"Squirrels are funny, eh?" the woman said, who wore a rain hat regardless of the weather. "Like us."

"Yes, even funnier. But I wonder if they ever get personal with each other."

"Get personal?" she ruminated. "Are you asking if they eat their nuts together? Perhaps before and after they hibernate."

"No, I mean, do they talk to one another about their problems? If one of them gets his tail caught in a fence. Or another one is paranoid about the hawks, do they share their problems and commiserate?"

"Oh, I see what you're getting at," the woman replied. "Are they empathetic? Maybe. I don't know. There isn't much clinical literature on the psychology of squirrels. Unfortunately."

"We humans listen to and discuss people's problems but I wonder why we bother if we can't solve them," I remarked.

The woman in the rain hat didn't immediately reply. But then she introduced herself. She explained that in her old country and in her old job she had been a psychiatrist. What good luck for me, I thought. However, what she said next had nothing to do with psychotherapy.

"I think there is a very good reason, a therapeutic reason for people to talk about their problems—and for others to listen. We all need someone to listen. It's not because we believe our difficulties will disappear like magic. We don't expect a solution—only acknowledgement. When you listen to another human being's distress you do them a great service. You give meaning to their pain by hearing about it.

"Nietzsche claimed that the Greeks invented gods not to relieve their suffering but to witness it and give it significance. Today we have no gods, so we witness one another's pain by paying attention when others speak of it."

I thanked the squirrel-feeding psychiatrist for listening to *me*. Her words encouraged me to "get personal" again if I ever encountered anyone who needed to talk. She helped me to realize that I had been thwarted by two opposing impulses—to protect myself from pain and to heroically make it disappear. I resolved to listen to others without judgment, not from a grandiose desire to reach into their lives and solve their dilemmas and debacles, but to acknowledge their misery and give it significance. We will never eliminate suffering but we can build a bridge to it with our hearts and minds so that no one endures it in isolation and silence.

THE FALLACY OF COMPETITION

Competition is like bacon in America—we put it on everything, even where it doesn't belong. We love sports because they are steeped in competition, but competition is also a major component of politics, where it has come to preclude compromise and collaboration regarding even the most serious matters, including our response to national emergencies.

We cannot seem to appreciate or derive meaning from any activity that does not produce a winner and a loser. We turn everything into a fight and rouse ourselves to high excitement when engaging in or spectating the violence. In the process, we often forget why we're competing. Competition becomes the condiment that overwhelms and transfigures everything we put it on.

Competition has insinuated itself in the arts, where contests abound in literature, music, fine art and dance. These contests have become qualifying events that shape the cultural landscape. Even cooking and baking have evolved from domestic arts to gladiatorial events. This may be a last ditch tactic to validate the arts for those who can only value them if they are derived from assessable criteria and produce quantifiable results.

The need to compete is addictive. From being only a part of our lives, it has consumed our lives. From making things a little more interesting, it has become the sole source of interest.

We learn to compete as children. Our culture presents competition as a virtue that produces the greatest good. We come to see it as a natural law, a universal fact of life, a biological and psychological necessity, as fundamental to living as breathing.

As a child, I competed for the love of my parents, the praise of my teachers, the friendship of my peers. There were grades, school elections, plays, sports teams and intramurals. Ironically, recess was the only time when competition nearly disappeared. Though we boys played touch football, basketball and capture-the-flag, we didn't care who won or lost.

In those blissful moments we were children running, playing and having fun. The fresh air, our intensity and laughter, and the dew of perspiration on our skins rinsed away the slime of competition. This was why we were so dejected when the teacher waved her arm to summon us back to class.

Though competition was as much a part of me as my breakfast cereal, by middle school, a counterforce in me resisted standard forms of competition as measures of my self worth. I sought a higher ground on which to compete beyond report cards and a mastery of school subjects. I discovered the aptitudes and interests I valued most in myself and decided to make them my "competitive edge." I even hoped they might propel me beyond the grueling cycle of competition.

In high school and college, I developed these abilities and aspirations until they became so ingrained and specific to me that I ceased to believe I was competing. At worst, I only competed against my aspirations.

But when I lived alone in the world in my tenement flat, I re-entered the competitive environment, though I told myself I was apart from it.

One evening I found myself out of my social and financial depth in a party of well-heeled people. A man ten years my senior and well established held forth. Amused by my unconventional style, he engaged me in a debate about competition. He maintained that everyone competed, whether they knew it and liked it or not.

I countered that no competition could occur if people refused to compete, or if they were so different that there was no basis for competition. But the guru of competition was tenacious.

"Even by being non-competitive, you're competing—with competitive people, that is," he declared. "When people are different, their differences compete. They're competitive strategies in the struggle for life."

The competition-guru rhapsodized like this all evening and by the end of it he made competition sound inexorable and downright Darwinian. He claimed that everyone competed in every conceivable manner. Ideologies, lifestyles, philosophies all competed. But how was a winner to be decided in all of this competition? He didn't say.

I resisted the gospel of the competition-meister but he had a strong point, which I realized when I focused on any career goal. At some point everyone, including me, wanted something others wanted, so we had to compete or be thrust into competition for it, often without perceiving our competitors.

This competitive reality not only applied to the coveted rewards of life. Scarcity dictated that regardless of what I wanted or needed, there was never enough of it and there were always others competing for it. Even apparently accessible goals became battles of attrition. When a day job in a sneaker store or a lunch counter was posted, many applied and only one person was hired.

I tried to negotiate between competing for survival and keeping the valued parts of myself out of the perpetual contest. Nonetheless, as I got older, competition imposed itself on my lifestyle, diet and even my sense of happiness. When I became a parent, I infected my daughter with it.

Once while we were walking to the park, my daughter was seven or eight at the time, she lamented that she wished she could go back to when she was two or three years old. I was surprised she said this because children are generally oriented to the future. If anything, they wish to be older, not younger. When I asked my daughter why she felt this way, she replied, "There was no competition then."

The relentless spirit of competition permeated every facet of my life, even when I believed I had no reason to compete. Then one day I had my reckoning with the competitive instinct.

At a café, I passed a table where an impecunious man studied lottery tickets spread out like Solitaire cards before him. He seemed to meditate on the flimsy paper rectangles as he pondered his next move on a game board only he could see. Or he was trying to impart luck to them with the power of his desire.

He looked so earnest and desperate that I spontaneously wished him good luck. The lottery player accepted my good wishes with a nod of his head and a wan smile, as if he barely believed his own chances, despite the fervent efforts he lavished on them.

This man's fixation on the spindled chits suggested that his circumstances were dire. Wishing the desperate Lotto player well was like giving money to a street musician. I was suffused with a wave of good feeling, a rare sensation of universal kinship. Just then, it was clear to me that every wish or deed for another person confirmed the best in me, that I acknowledged and cared about others, since we were essentially alike.

My casual remark ought to have ended on that note, but wishing good luck to the desperate lottery player suddenly struck me as capricious and irresponsible since I had played numbers in the same drawing.

Did I violate my self-interest by wishing luck to a competitor? The lottery law was unequivocal: only one set of numbers would win; unless we had identical numbers, an unlikely outcome, his win would mean my loss.

The implications of wishing another lottery player good luck proliferated as I pondered them. Such incongruous bonhomie implied the resignation of a failing spirit, even a diminished interest in life—and a premature concession of defeat.

The twisted spirit of competition now flared up in me and was ripping me apart. The tourniquet of reason needed to be applied. I told myself that my passing remark was a superficial pleasantry or a wry ironic wisecrack, since we were both likely losers.

I did not believe I controlled anything with good will. Yet wishing an adversary good luck before a contest violated the essence of competition. It signified supreme arrogance—like I did not expect to lose—or a contemptible lack of faith—like I did not expect to win.

Then I stopped myself. "What does competition have to do with the lottery?" I asked. "It's a game and there are only a few winners, but we choose numbers on a hunch or let a machine select them for us. In what sense are we competing?"

I had no answer until a thought came to me that changed my life. I realized that a lottery was a synthesis and metaphor for every other crucial game in life. While there were winners and losers, the lottery wasn't truly competitive because there was no criterion for winning.

It was a matter of scale. In a lottery, where winning was miraculous and losing was the norm, the rules of competition were mitigated and deviated. Perhaps competition, like sub-atomic particles, obeyed different rules as the possibility of winning grew smaller and more remote. It also seemed plausible that the spirit of competition took hold only when the possibility to win was tangible.

However, if competition were such a powerful drive, no minimum floor or maximum ceiling would contain it, and our negligible prospect of victory ought to have been irrelevant. An Everest of anecdotes supports this point: on one end, a billionaire fights with another over a paltry point of pride; on the other, a brother slays another over "chump change."

Yet we lottery players entered a new universe where normal rules of competition apparently no longer applied. We played a no-compete game. We were connected to a colossal spinning wheel and a universal aspiration for freedom from a *samsara* of pain. The stakes were so high and our probability of winning so low that we were like particles floating along tenuous, yet powerful force lines. Our proximity was physical and cultural but illusory, since our destinies were and would remain infinitely apart.

It struck me that when stochastic forces like luck, life and death are in play, competition no longer applies. We go shoulder to shoulder against a coalition of implacable nemeses—disease, scarcity, uncertainty, and indifference—driven by fear and emboldened by our collective strength.

If my friendly wish for the other lottery player's success did not align with a lifetime of thinking first and foremost of myself, it was because competition did not pertain to us and the game we played. We were not opposing gladiators but commiserating stiffs.

I conducted a thought experiment. I imagined there were only two people left in the world—the lottery machine operator and me. I realized that even if I were the only player, without competitors, my odds of winning the game would not improve.

The lottery was a game but not a competition. The millions of players were there to sweeten the pot. We did not confront one another but an implacable, impersonal adversary. In matters of luck, competition is not a factor. My luck is my own—as friend, foe or oblivious bystander.

Similarly, in matters of health, statistics show that half of all men will have erectile dysfunction by age 50, one in ten will have prostate cancer, and one in four men and women will have a form of arthritis, yet my health outcomes are irrelevant to the next person's. We do not compete in health. By the same token, if one in two marriages ends in divorce, the next couple's happy marriage does not require my divorce.

Banausic struggles for scarce resources, like parking on a city street, can also be mistaken for competition. In this familiar scenario, fraught with nerve-wracking obstacles, putative competitors cruise residential streets—stopping, starting, accelerating, weaving and turning. Yet, despite our diverse stratagems, we only ostensibly compete since a car vacates a space unpredictably. In such erratic circumstances, all tactics are nullified and luck is more determinative than experience, logic and time expended at the task. A naïve driver who enters a neighborhood clueless about how to play this game may find the next space by being in precisely the right place at the right time.

We are told that we ought to compete for the world's goods but this is a canard. What is most significant in our lives we cannot compete for, even if we want to. In terms of our families, upbringing, education, how we think, look and behave, we compete with no one but an ideal.

Yet the non-competitive nature of all that is important in life, a reality that ought to bind us, results in vexation and anxiety, not contentment and release. Equality disorients and disarms us. We may feel that it stifles our individuality. We are so determined to establish our value, to rise above all others who are level with us, that we play gratuitous games of competition to tell us who we are and where we are. Otherwise we fear we're nowhere.

The fallacy of competition disguises the hard wiring of our fates. It offers the illusion that we can reverse the indeterminacy and randomness at the core of our lives. We believe winning confers certainty, honor, beauty, strength, power, bliss, greatness and *transcendence*. The promise of surpassing the cruelty and banality of existence through controlled and endless conflict is enough to offset for many the unremitting violence and bitterness of competition—and its lack of finality.

SPEED TRAP:
THE FALLACY OF LOCAL VS. EXPRESS

One late afternoon after a rainstorm, I was driving toward the George Washington Bridge, one of three conduits linking New York City with the mainland, when I came to a familiar fork in the highway that offered a simple choice—Express or Local.

An overhead sign with an arrow and the message "Best Route" was always lit to suggest the faster alternative to the bridge. That afternoon the arrow pointed, per usual, to the local lanes. The arrow appeared to be stuck and was not to be trusted. I speculated that the arrow indicated "local" because the Turnpike Authority preferred motorists to take local lanes for capricious motives of their own, not to help drivers save time or improve traffic flow.

"Express" always sounds faster than "local" and its reputation often matches the experience. Unless you have nothing to do and nowhere to go, you will take an express train over a local 99 times out of 100—unless you need a local stop.

At the split on Route 95 North, the express and local lanes diverge and arc away from a driver's sight lines, suggesting equal speed and convenience. On this late afternoon, both ramps seemed fast and lightly traveled, so I took the express lane and sped up the gradient and around the bend. My mind was awash in distractions, careering on its own oblique path, and I did not realize I was on the verge of an epiphany that would change my decision-making process and self-perception.

Just beyond the curve, I discovered that traffic in the express lane was at a standstill for miles ahead. I had been fooled into selecting the express route, which is presumed to be faster since it permits no exits. My shallow interpretation of "express" (express=faster) would now cost me two precious hours of my life.

I had faced this debacle before, (few experiences occur once), but had forgotten the same prior adverse outcomes of taking the "express" route. Even so, my reflexive decision was not careless or baseless. I stood on solid

115

empirical ground. Like many poor decisions, this one had masqueraded as a good one, producing acceptable results in a large number of tries; a few poor outcomes had been buried under a preponderance of positive data.

Two hours was a long time to fume over an idling motor. While I sat helplessly in the motorized morass, with vehicles in the local lanes speeding by on the local side of the guardrails that barred my freedom, I felt deceived by an example of double-speak, in which *local* was fast and *express* was slow. It reeked of a conspiracy to confuse and torture the public. No doubt, a cabal of engineers had devised a practical joke and now enjoyed a hearty laugh at our expense.

However, as dusk descended, it dawned on me that a conspiracy of pranking engineers was implausible. Instead, this was another example of language not keeping pace with facts. I put my faith in a word—*express*—without accounting for the reality of a super-highway, where "express" simply meant "no egress." Express lanes seemed faster, more direct and more efficient because no one could leave or enter them, but their "no escape" clause did not preclude stagnation.

The implications of *express* ought to have been clear to me. Speed and efficiency are inconsistent with freedom and choice. I failed to think through the premise—and the promise—of express. In theory, you move faster when you can't opt out. And since I was going straight home, I didn't believe I needed exits, choices or connections with local roads. I had suffered a misconception—that it was ever a safe bet to trade off freedom for expediency.

Everyone moving in one direction without alternatives and exceptions can work under optimal conditions. If motorists must move forward, they cannot indulge second thoughts, slow down or stop the flow. However, when a blockage lies ahead, no exit means no way forward and no way out—no way to drain congestion, reduce volume and increase the flow. The streamlined exclusivity of the express lanes made them the ultimate speed trap.

Granted, freedom has limits. Local lanes allow one to egress into back roads, but in the end, one must still re-enter the highway and sit in traffic at the toll plaza and on the bridge. In such circumstances, one can turn, circle and zigzag for a small advantage and spend 29 minutes to save a half-hour. Even so, one is better off *psychologically* by taking action than by being trapped.

Freedom is our most basic insurance. When entering a highway or a room, I make a point of knowing the exits. As I endured this traffic debacle, I vowed never to take the express route again, regardless of how fast and empty it might seem, since the promise of speed without freedom was patently worthless. The route with most options for escape would always be superior since accidents are routine and delay is more likely than not. I now recognized that express without egress comes with disproportionate risk and inadequate reward.

Thinking beyond the specific driving lessons of this experience, I wondered how often I had been deceived by the flashy promises of a faster track. How often had I believed I was saving time when I was losing it, that I was on the right path when I was on the wrong one, that I was taking a shortcut that sent me on a long road to nowhere?

As I sat in the inert car, I challenged the notion that this situation was out of my control. I had been mindlessly naïve about the express lane. I should have known better but I was seduced as always by the promise of getting somewhere faster.

There were no shortcuts or express lanes in life but I wanted to believe in them. Saving time was like finding gold—an activity inducing a rush of exhilarating hope that often resulted in crashing failure. As I inched closer to the tollbooths amid a scrum of belching vehicles, I reflected with much head shaking on the many times I had been misled by my passion for the fast lane. I skipped junior year of high school and entered college as an immature 17-year-old, a self-imposed disadvantage from which I eventually recovered. Later I left the Peace Corps after one year rather than two, only to rush to New York during a recession.

Nor were these errors of impetuous youth. Regardless of age and experience, or the personal significance of what I was doing, my attitude toward speed never changed. In my urgent haste to be published, I often submitted manuscripts with mistakes. I handled my social life in a similar manner, rushing impatiently from parties before they had a chance to get started. Even when I "settled down" in a career, I was constantly restless and ready to move on, often leaving one job for another with a better title or a slightly higher income, but offering no greater fulfillment or security. How many roads had I exited prematurely only to meander anxiously on secondary byways, ultimately arriving late to my destination? My life was apparently a litany of addiction to the express lane.

In a fever of self-awareness, I rebuked myself for a lifetime of mistaking speed for freedom, although poor judgment was not entirely to blame. Speed *is* exhilarating. When we move fast, we experience a rush of adrenaline-induced euphoria, which is not freedom, but a chemical rush we often mistake for it. Freedom is a more secure feeling that comes with the acknowledgement of options.

When I arrived home, my wife asked why I was despondent.

"I got stuck in the express lane."

"That's all? It happens. At least you're home now."

"I realized my life is ruined."

She looked at me quizzically but she was used to my exaggerations.

"You mean your evening was ruined."

I sighed and regarded her dolefully. How could I explain to her what I had discovered while going nowhere in the express lane? It would take time, which was precisely what I always seemed to lack. On the other hand, didn't my time concerns make me late?

"I'm always taking short-cuts, working fast and trying to be efficient to save time—but it never works. I save a minute and lose an hour," I said.

She smiled. "Don't blame yourself for trying. Time is all we have."

"Yes, that's what I tell myself," I replied as I felt a bit brighter. "Even so, I'm going to stop saving time."

We agreed it was a good idea, then sat down to dinner and had a fine evening.

MY MALADIES

Risk is not my forte. I don't sail, ski, climb or dive. I don't even like to travel. I am more inclined to cultivate habits than set off on adventures, so the only frontier I'm likely to explore in my lifetime is my body—how it feels, what it can do and how I can improve its function.

My limitations in this endeavor are apparent. I am as ill-equipped to explore the dark interior of my body as I am to wander rainforests and desert canyons. Physicians and researchers are the certified voyagers in this corps of discovery.

Medical mariners navigate strange waters—blood, lymph and other body fluids. They reconnoiter familiar domains, such as organs, bones and muscles, as well as remote microenvironments, where cells crosstalk and interact. They witness mysterious processes they can neither verbalize nor fully comprehend. However, clinicians are not amateur adventurers. They explore in order to nullify hostile agents with the standard and experimental therapies at their disposal.

Patients must also participate in this quest. Though we lack the tools to evaluate what signs and symptoms mean, we see and feel disease firsthand. Physicians can only guess at the significance and origins of the ailments we describe, which may be undetectable on diagnostic machines.

Medical mysteries are a popular subject of speculation and entertainment. They often pertain to rare and extreme conditions that produce hideous and terrifying effects. Yet the vast majority of unknown and undiagnosed diseases are the kind we endure and do not report to our doctors because they come and go, and are as specific to our identities as our respective families and routines.

Meanwhile, the medical community we depend upon and trust cannot keep pace with the microbes that cause these maladies, because through their own inscrutable bonds and communications, these microorganisms share information and defenses against the weapons we deploy against them. Bacteria become resistant and viruses mutate before researchers can give them proper names. Humans believe we're smart but microbes are the true geniuses—and they don't have brains.

What makes our health more difficult to track is that our bodies are the part of us that remain infantile in their ability to communicate. Bodies experience many things but they cannot tell us what they're feeling because they have extremely limited means of doing so. They do not speak, so much as ache, swell, feel sharp pain, burn with fever and shake with chills.

Even lingering diseases can be so peculiar and unique that they seem to have been custom-made for us. How often has my primary care physician declared that my symptoms were "soft," ambiguous, and hard to diagnose? I have been told that I would need to undergo a battery of tests, which might prove inconclusive, since they are designed to identify known antigens and markers, not to discover new ones. Even when symptoms arrange themselves in a pattern, their cause is often classified as idiopathic, i.e. unknown.

Ultimately, in the frontier of one's own body and well-being, each pioneer must explore and discover alone and defend oneself as the need arises. Confronted by a vast universe of microbes and cellular interactions, most of which is unknown to the medical profession, each patient must carefully monitor his or her health and find a pattern among an array of baffling symptoms to arrive at a diagnosis. Then, with a restricted protocol and limited supplies, one must devise a treatment plan of unproven efficacy.

This brief account of three of my strange illnesses is not meant to elicit sympathy. It is not my "war story" in the trenches of infection and inflammation. It is written, rather, in the spirit of information and discovery, as a field report by someone who has wandered in a viral wilderness and emerged from it with detailed notes.

I've been a beneficiary of robust health for much of my life, yet I've never mistakenly believed I was the sole occupant of my body. I do not view myself as anything more than its landlord and majority shareholder.

This complex and mysterious vessel I live in is more like a transient hotel than a private estate and it shelters a diverse range of residents. Some are benign but none would I call savory. For instance, at any moment, several millions of staphylococcus bacteria hover like an invisible sheath over every square inch of my newly showered skin, ready for the slightest opportunity—a nick, a cut, a scrape, a weakness in immunity—to break in.

At the same time, my gut would not work without powerful flora, which, if released through a breach in my intestinal tract, could kill me.

But even a healthy body can't dodge every bad character. From time to time, my microbial boarding house receives a harmful guest.

There is a special visitor that comes around my body once a year. It is my "special virus" because I doubt any clinician could give it a name or identify one other person who shares with me the pathogenesis of this disease and its particular sequence of signs and symptoms.

My special virus is far from sentimental, yet it shows me perverse consideration. It comes in early February, as if to celebrate my birthday, then stays with me—or inside me—for a month. It always seems to take the red-eye because it shows up without warning in the dead of the night. Because of its peculiar timing around my birthday, I named it FEBVID.

This is what it's like.

I wake up at 4AM knowing something, *everything*, is wrong. I swallow hard and feel a thickening in my throat that will not be relieved, regardless of how often I clear it.

At first, I forget what time of year it is, that my virus is due to visit and always arrives at night. In the first disorienting moments of discomfort after my eyes snap open, my immediate response is that this weird feeling must stop. But I know it won't.

I'm trapped, scared and agitated. I can't rest or relax because my body won't let me. It is out of sorts and out of control. Something insidious has taken over and I've been reduced to a bystander.

The thick and swollen sensation in my throat worries me. It feels like my trachea is closing. I feel like I may stop breathing. I start to panic. How can I go on like this or get through the night? One thought poises me. I tell myself, "You're not dying."

I've had this virus before but I never get so used to it that I greet its arrival blandly, "Oh, it's you again!" It so swiftly and decisively alters how I feel that I lie awake, thinking, "What is it? *Not this again.* I can't bear it."

Soon my throat hurts. I want to close my eyes, ignore it and return to sleep but I can't lie still. A voice in my head tells me not to call an ambulance or awaken my wife. This inner voice reproves me for exaggerating my peril, advises me to be calm, and reassures me that I can take simple measures to feel better. Momentum shifts from the disease to the healer in me. My confidence is being restored.

I spring from bed, pace the bedroom and consider my options. Maybe I need a glass of water to dilute the mucus shellacking my throat. I drink but the cold water does nothing to alleviate the swollen throat. I swallow two *Advils*, spray my throat with antiseptic, lie down and wait for sleep.

"It's only a virus," I reassure myself. "You can handle this."

I start to feel better. Sleep comes. This has not been an unprecedented attack but something familiar I can handle. My life enters a new normal.

Now that I'm sure my virus has returned like the swallows to Capistrano, I need to accept a new, temporary level of wellness. I accommodate myself to aggravating symptoms in the same forbearing way that I deal with environmental inconveniences like street construction. This will become my new health for weeks or even a month.

This bug causes mild, flu-like symptoms, for which the sore throat is the overture. Within a few days I run the gamut: fatigue, irritability, weakness, body pain, nausea and dizziness all make their appearances and fade. The virus proceeds to move up and down my body, plaguing my sinuses, my head, my gut and joints, before wracking me with a hacking cough.

Then, like a mercurial houseguest who capriciously goes sightseeing, FEBVID disappears. I feel better for a day or two until it returns with a new symptom.

There is no known vaccine, cure or name for FEBVID. It is a birthday malady that comes as a spiteful gift to my healthy existence, or as a tax I pay to my flawed humanity.

FEBVID is a clever pathogen. It knows how much I despise lying in bed immobilized, so it grants me sufficient energy to move around. It lets me feel stronger through the day until I relapse at night.

My special virus plays with my head as well as my body. Our relationship is symbiotic. It keeps me on my feet for its own benefit. As long as I go about my routine, I am potentially spreading it in every breath I exhale. In this way, FEBVID uses me as its home and vehicle until one day it dies inside me or flees to find more action.

I don't immediately realize that the virus is gone. My army of antibodies has not only evicted the malady but numbed my perceptions of it with its wartime propaganda. As my hacking cough has pummeled me, my immune system has inured me to it by telling me the cough was normal.

Anyone who has witnessed or experienced more serious maladies will shrug at FEBVID. But FEBVID is only the opening act for another illness I endured that presented bizarre symptoms and for which modern medicine also has no name or cure.

Versatility and mobility are successful adaptations for the modern pathogen and a flu-like virus that attacks the upper respiratory and GI tracts is not unusual. However, another bug I recently hosted was more evolved. It tramped through my body like an itinerant army, plundering every hamlet in its path.

This mercurial adversary was a cunning question mark, not satisfied to take the well-traveled pathways of less enterprising viruses like FEBVID. It was a protean shape-shifter that wreaked havoc in various places one never associates with viral infections.

The anonymous infection first presented as a pain in the neck before recurring as a stiff back, sore shoulders, creaking knees and a swollen toe. Eventually one side of my body ached. This was a Lon Chaney of pathogens, a master of disguise giving a bravura performance.

By attacking so many places on my body—but never in the nose, throat or lungs—this virus concealed its identity and feigned its probable causes. The stiff neck seemed to result from a draft. The tight lower back was like a spasm presumably caused by bending or reaching awkwardly. The afflicted big toe felt like I'd stubbed it, while the throbbing knee mimicked osteoarthritis, aging's notorious companion.

While it tortured my body, this master psychologist toyed with my mind. It was a guerilla illness that darted from one spot to another, presenting itself as many unrelated problems, so that I would not know what I had and how to treat it. Eventually, I was overwhelmed by the multiplicity of ailments and believed my body was falling apart.

But the cunning infection finally revealed its viral identity when it presented as bursitis. It produced sharp discomfort at the top of the shoulder at the nexus of the collarbone, which limited my arm motion above my chest. However, it did not prevent me from swimming or moving my arm otherwise, as bursitis would have done. (Bursitis typically affects the shoulder at a lower point and renders all arm motion painful and impossible.) This variance in mobility and location confirmed that I had no sports injury, but a viral imposter.

With movement and disguise and by attacking muscles and joints, rather than the respiratory and GI systems, this novel virus perpetuated itself by being hard to diagnose. Like FEBVID, it kept me off balance by seeming to disappear, only to return to a previous location. By coming and going, it undermined my morale and shifted my perspective from treatment to coping.

We carry diseases clinicians have never seen and named, much less diagnosed or treated. If you describe your symptoms to a physician, you can often expect no more than a shrug, since chances are that he has never seen your illness before. Familiar disorders can lay you low, but the misery of physical signs is exacerbated when your ailment is novel and untreatable.

For this reason, a patient with a novel disease with a unique symptom set should be able to report it on a patient registry. Such a registry would be a resource for other sufferers to identify similar signs and symptoms. It would also help patients dispel uncertainties that can turn a mystifying illness into an emotional storm. Someone who feels ill should not be made to feel insane as well.

Even widespread and debilitating disorders with well-documented and observable signs, symptoms and prognoses often have mysterious and unknown causes. These idiopathic diseases include inflammatory conditions, like rheumatoid arthritis and Crohn's disease. Just as these disorders appear suddenly and originate in perplexing ways, the therapies prescribed to treat them often have unknown mechanisms of action. When the drugs work no one can say why.

I had a baffling illness a few years ago that scared and depressed me. I was in a slump at the time and thought I could feel no worse. Work was hard to find and I worried over money. Then in the middle of this morass, out of nowhere, I was stricken by an odd, debilitating malady. At first, my back ached, then my knees. I dismissed these symptoms as commonplace—a twist here, an awkward movement there. I might have wrenched my knee running down stairs and strained my back in my sleep.

Then early one morning, when only the dog-walkers were out, I received a call from a Good Samaritan who had found my cell phone on a patch of grass near my car. When I put on clothes to meet this kind stranger and retrieve my phone, I realized my feet were badly swollen. I could barely walk or fit them into shoes. A few days later, my wrist began to ache. I tried to allay the persistent pain with massage, anti-inflammatory medicines and a brace, but nothing worked. Just as I was learning to live with the inflamed wrist, the pain migrated to my shoulders and I could barely push open a door or turn a steering wheel.

Weeks later, prior anxieties over a lack of work seemed risible and irrelevant. I knew I was in no shape to do much of anything. Would I ever function normally again? An inexplicable and disabling illness had put me in a new reality, where normal activities, duties, habits and plans were no longer germane. The illness debilitated my body and usurped my will.

I resorted to every over-the-counter remedy and gave my body time to heal but after more than a month of suffering, I stopped toughing it out and saw my family physician. I'll never forget the look on his face when I removed my shoes and socks. He handled and studied my swollen feet and exclaimed, "Eric!" He was a veteran physician and had seen his share of lumps, lesions and suspect swellings during a long practice, yet he appeared unsettled by the gravity of my unexpected inflammation.

For years, I had been an outlier in his practice, a patient in apparently indomitable good health. I had never presented this degree of illness. He regarded me differently now, as if I were finally worthy of his medical skill. His eyes evinced the same compassion he must have shown to his aged Medicare patients with their chronic, incurable suffering that exceeded every remedy but palliation. His changed manner scared me more than anything else. In his view, I finally needed his care.

The physician took a blood sample and ordered tests. When he phoned with the results, his voice was gravid with bad news. He said there was a high level of C-reactive proteins and antinuclear antibodies in my blood. He urged me to see a rheumatologist.

However, I wasn't prepared to face a diagnosis of rheumatoid arthritis, lupus or another inflammatory disease. I knew autoimmune diseases were incurable and degenerative and constituted a life sentence. They might not kill me like cancer, but they would turn my body into a prison and torture chamber that would steal my freedom and punish the simplest motion and activity. Worse, the drugs that treated inflammatory disorders were toxic and would suppress my immune system, making me susceptible to other serious diseases, including lymphoma.

Based on how the past six weeks had gone I knew this disease would not go away or let up. All of the braces and bandages I obtained to alleviate the pain were strewn around my bedroom like used Band-Aids. My life was laid out before me like an examination table or a bloody red carpet. I would languish, connected to IV bags and poles, infusing biologics that would open my body to tuberculosis and cancer. I recoiled from this likely fate. I knew I had to try another way.

126

Rather than see a rheumatologist, as my physician advised, I consulted with an orthopedist who had treated me before for wrist pain diagnosed as tenosynovitis—a local inflammation of a tendon sheath in the wrist. This time, I complained of wrist pain, but never mentioned the joint pain in my shoulder, the throbbing knees and swollen feet. As far as the hand specialist knew, the inflammation was only in my wrist. He examined my hand, determined I had tenosynovitis and administered the cortisone injection that had resolved it before. It was supposed to work only locally, but in 24 hours I was completely better.

I probably should have been satisfied to feel normal again but I remained curious about why I was ill in the first place. The blood work indicated an inflammatory disorder and I needed to know more about it.

I had made an appointment with a rheumatologist on the advice of my family doctor. Now that I felt better, the truth couldn't hurt me, so I kept the appointment to obtain information and closure. In the waiting room an elderly woman sat alone on a couch next to an IV pole. She was receiving an infusion through a tube in her arm—it was the horrific fate I had envisioned for myself.

The rheumatologist sensed that I came for answers and was quick to provide one. He said I had *palindromic rheumatism,* a rare form of rheumatoid arthritis that flared up sporadically for unknown reasons and left without causing joint damage. Palindromic rheumatism got its name because it attacked joints of the body in a certain order and left them in reverse order like a palindrome. There was no test to confirm its diagnosis.

It was satisfying to know the name and pathophysiology of this quirky yet terrifying illness that followed a pattern and afflicted every patient differently. I felt lucky because palindromic rheumatism was a relatively benign arthritis: it did not impair me for life and it never returned. But it also never left my mind. I know it can knock on my joints at any time—and a part of me expects it to return.

If it does, I won't welcome it, but at least I'll know what it is.

BEING MY OWN MASSEUR

It is a mundane injustice that insincere statements can be true. For instance, how many times have you heard someone say, "At least you have your health?" I used to hear this bromide frequently (presumably because I seemed to have little but my health) and it always translated in my mind as, "You're a loser but at least you can breathe, so it could be worse."

Deep down I suspected that these consolatory words were meant to shut me up. I never thought for a second that I would one day agree with them. Health *is* precious and a threat to it induces a relentless, grinding fear. Conversely, when we fall ill due to mysterious causes and then regain our health, the ordeal may imbue us with fresh confidence and strength.

A few years ago, my orthopedist prescribed a non-invasive, non-pharmacological, self-help treatment for my ailing shoulder: eight sessions with a physical therapist whose offices were in an upscale health club.

It was like a spa. How luxurious it was for someone to lay hands on my aching joints, to have hot, moist towels applied, a regimen of exercises to accomplish and a refreshing ice pack at the end to deep-freeze the inflammation. This experience was so "old-world" that I felt transported to a Hemingway short story from World War I, updated with continuous satellite radio and women in designer active sportswear.

This therapy was also wondrous for its simplicity. The tools of the physical therapist are for the most part as ancient and effective as chicken soup, cupping, bed rest and love, itself. I leaned on a wall, tugged many times on a brightly colored rubber band, tossed a ball and lifted a barbell. It was low-tech and direct but like a good old-fashioned breakfast, it made me feel so much better than I expected.

Four years later my shoulder "impingement" recurred after a long bout of non-specific inflammation that jumped from one joint to another for six weeks until it found a home in the knot of muscles in my upper arm. Money was tighter, my health plan was parsimonious and the prospect of even a series of $20 co-pays to a family physician, an orthopedist and a physical therapist was no longer feasible.

Frugality prompted a radical initiative: why should I not become my own physical therapist? I decided one evening to use my right hand to knead the aching triceps of my left arm, which felt like it had been punched repeatedly very hard.

Massaging myself seemed eccentric, desperate and not therapeutically promising. I was acutely aware of its implications. Embedded in the meaning of "care" is to be cared for by someone else. Auto-massage might come across as therapeutic masturbation or a pathetic sign of social marginality. Its effectiveness was also suspect. Regardless of behavioral taboo, we observe strict conventions regarding professional services. Self-healing, like acting as one's own attorney, seems imprudent and self-defeating.

This psychological baggage had to be unpacked and disposed of before I could give myself the therapy I needed. The physical part came easier. My strong right hand on my aching left triceps and shoulder worked well enough, which was not surprising, since I was a good amateur masseur dating back to college. However, at that time I never viewed this talent as "legitimate," since I used my youthful hands and therapeutic bent to seduce women rather than to heal them—not technically a transgression, yet probably not what Hippocrates had in mind.

I was a one-handed masseur but what an intelligent hand it was! It knew where the muscle hurt and how to press the injured area in just the right way to promote blood flow and stimulate healing. I had been no fool to be my own therapist; in addition to the beneficial physical impact I was having came the satisfaction of self-reliance.

Yet, when I had finished the massage, my self-treatment remained incomplete. Two embellishments were essential to provide a satisfying therapeutic experience—hot, moist towels to start the therapy and an ice pack to conclude it.

On one level, the moist heat and ice cold had seemed to be public relations gestures, like a clinician's white coat. They lent the imprimatur of science to physical therapy and made a patient believe the treatment was efficacious. As commercial flourishes, hot towels and ice packs offered a modicum of luxury and comfort, like fresh linen in a hotel.

Yet even if hot towels and ice packs resemble props, they are not adventitious frills but integral to therapy. With the exception of one expert massage I received, hot towels and ice packs were the aspect of treatment I liked best. I marveled at the simplicity of these amenities, yet I never felt cheated by them, as I would have been by a grandiose décor at an upscale restaurant, where finesse often distracts from the quality of the product rather than improving it.

Hot towels and ice could be obtained anywhere. These commonplace items required little skill and no technology to prepare, yet I expected and looked forward to them. They were not merely effective, but gratifying insofar as they fulfilled my craving for the ritual of healing. Therapeutically, hot towels and ice provided comfort, while, spiritually, they established the context in which recovery seemed possible. They instilled belief.

Healthcare has implicit religious overtones. The protocols of healing comprise a liturgy of significant moments and symbolic gestures: a doctor's admonition to move this and flex that, the tapping of ribs, the rubbing of anesthetic on an injection site, the drawing of dark blood through vermicelli-thin tubes into glass vials. These perfunctory clinical tasks achieve clinical objectives but have potent psychological effects. Medical care fulfills a requirement of ritual: symbolically, it transports a patient from the world he came from to a new state when it is over.

Hot towels and ice packs marked the prologue and coda of my ritual of physical therapy. They indicated that I was entering and leaving a sacred space. Hot towels at the threshold of the event removed me from the hard surfaces and rough jostling of the world by assuaging its abuses, while the ice pack after rigorous exercise modified the stimulation and inflammation induced by therapy and conveyed me back to my daily life.

In my home version of physical therapy, I had plied the technical skill of massage on my body while depriving myself of the threshold pleasures of hot towels and ice. I might have committed this oversight out of a deep-seated distaste for domesticity. Soothing tight muscles and aching joints with my hands seemed a prestigious skill, whereas preparing ice packs and hot towels signified menial labor.

I had to overcome this qualm to obtain the full benefit of my self-care. I soaked several washcloths in hot water, wrung and stacked them, then placed them on my sore arm. When my self-massage was over, I applied an icepack to my arm until it tingled with numbness and the skin burned. Only then was I satisfied that my home therapy was complete.

Physicians and the insurance industry have underscored wellness, fitness and awareness as effective disease prevention strategies. These variations of self-care do not subvert medical professionals; they are intended to assist and relieve them. Doctors are overwhelmed by the number of patients they treat. They must welcome a health-conscious person like me, who utilizes fewer health resources by caring for himself.

Self-care empowers patients to improve and maintain their well-being. It tacitly acknowledges that patients must prevent many health problems since health resources are scarce and expensive. This reality cuts both ways. Most of us lack the time, money and access to seek attention for every ache, pain, chill and fever we experience. A popular adage is turned on its head: *Patient heal thyself.*

Everyone can and ought to learn self-healing even in a small way. Knowing one's body and how to care for it are key to self-reliance and self-love. We need to be attentive and to rely on our experience—not every problem can be solved this way, but many can. To start, we must view our bodies not just as our property to use and abuse but as living things entrusted to us. When I became my own masseur, the only attribute I could trust to compensate for the training I lacked was the knowledge I had of my body and my love for it. They made a vital difference.

Individualism, freedom and self-love are ideas that motivate the world, yet they are empty terms without self-knowledge and self-care. Ego may determine our next move but it will never sustain us for a long race. To love others, we must first love ourselves. There is no higher expression of such love than promoting our own good health.

THE ONES WHO HATED ME

It's understandable but not commendable that I recall the one person who hated me more vividly than the hundreds who liked me. I should not publicly acknowledge that I file my social media "likes" in special folders, like a human squirrel burying nuts for a needy day. If I didn't, I might forget that anyone *ever* liked me. Such measures are unnecessary with the ones who hated me. Their faces, names and characteristics are on wanted posters tacked to a bulletin board in my hippocampus.

I recently reflected on my teaching career and one student's name and face immediately came to mind. He was in my class for one semester, yet I still remember his major—hotel management—and his home state–Nebraska. He wore wire-rimmed glasses, had a pale, angular physiognomy and an intelligent air, though his coursework was unremarkable. He was never any trouble; to the contrary, he was polite. He did his work on time and came to class punctually and consistently. What distinguished this student from his peers and from all other students that semester and every other year was that he clearly and unequivocally hated me.

His acrimony is hard to forget. It was cold, passive but as obvious as the needles on a cactus. He showed his rancor in a hard look that he had no compunction to disguise. He knew the demonstration of his hostility was safe; what could I do or say about the look in a student's eyes?

Other students had disliked me more openly and offensively but less purely, less completely. They made their hostility apparent by showing up late for class, by making vituperative remarks, by arguing loudly, by questioning my credentials, and by probing for holes in my logic. By contrast, this student kept his loathing in check. He refused to give me an opportunity to get even. He issued no outbursts, uttered no insults, and performed no rude acts. He simply looked at me with remote hostility and answered questions as if to say that he would never credit my response. His presence in my class was compelled by fate and university requirements but he turned his enrollment into a dignified, silent protest.

I had no recourse but to try winning him over with cordiality to match his own and fairness to neutralize his tacit prejudice. Failing that, I encountered and absorbed his hatred every day.

Others have since joined this bland belligerent in the ranks of those who have loathed me, at times with financial consequences. In particular, one woman's face stares at me implacably. We were once colleagues but never worked together. On occasions we chatted amiably about personal matters; I know this because I still recall her husband's occupation, though I never met him. She and I had not one harsh word between us, yet I hear her voice in my head, inaudibly warning me, "I wouldn't give you the time of day if it were your last second on Earth." She hates me and wherever she works as a hiring manager, I know I will never get a job.

Why do I recollect these few individuals whose dislike for me was pure and baseless while I easily forget the many who have liked me?

Hatred, more than love, jolts and surprises us. It is as fascinating as a riddle, a disfigurement or a venomous reptile. It signals danger, warning us that a friend, acquaintance or stranger is actually a foe who might cause us harm. Hatred also gives us a perspective on ourselves which love renders inaccessible. It indicates that someone sees us as vile for reasons unknown and immutable. Unaccountable hatred declares one's existence superfluous and objectionable. It asks, "Why do we breathe the same air?"

Why do I dwell on such negation? It is humbling, yet I don't wish to be humbled in this way. Perhaps my fixation with the ones who hated me is associated with the primal fear of and attraction to death. Hatred is compelling and repulsive at once. It can kill you if the circumstances are right.

Hatred is a confounding mystery that won't be solved. It is the yellow tape that tells me where I must not go. Worse, it gainsays how I feel about myself. How is it possible that the individual who despises me does not see that I am lovable, likeable or at least worthwhile? This is one of the hardest facts to learn, handle or accept in the struggle to survive—the implacable and intractable presence of natural enemies.

POWER IS ABSOLUTE—IN THE MOMENT

We live in a republic but life is not a democracy. Rather, it is a series of tyrannies, large and small, that start at birth and early childhood, proceed to mandatory schooling and work, meander through an interminable protocol of rules, laws, duties and obligations, and then culminate in compulsory retirement and the final tyranny—death. There is little we can do to check, channel or divert this inexorable stream. We can only navigate it.

Democracy is a wish, an aspiration, a projection of our longing, while the vote, a symbolic democratic gesture, is our consolation prize to compensate for the despotism that rules our quotidian lives. We wish we could always pull a lever for the better of two outcomes. We wish we could resolve problems through negotiation and compromise from a position of equality, but life is not structured this way.

Power determines even our most exiguous interactions, and in even trace amounts, power is absolute. Rather than make our voices heard, we are frequently admonished to be quiet. Our eloquence can betray us and our words become quicksand when we are under the absolute power of others. Assertion and aggression are futile when we depend on their judgment.

Society is regulated by the meting out of power in discrete units among a vast number of people—many of whom we never meet or see. Power is discharged and circulated constantly and continuously like blood pumping through the amebic body of society. It structures our lives as it tells us what our next move should be to appease or avoid it.

We don't often view power as so widely and mundanely disseminated. Rather, power has the aura of a rare and glamorous substance, the social, interactive equivalent of gold. It is primarily symbolic for most of us, much of the time. We consider it a status ornament, not the dull, utile instrument it is. Power can seem as remote to us as the gilded lives of celebrities and billionaires that are never far from our sight. Such power we believe is of little concern to us, since we are unlikely to directly encounter it.

Such mythic power is a resource amassed and controlled by a well-organized elite cadre of like-minded individuals. According to this model, human power resembles electric power, a mysterious and awesome current surging through conduits as deadly and familiar as power cables, yet organized in a format as unobtrusive and pervasive as an energy grid.

Our corporate culture and conspiracy fixation reinforce the notion of power as a sublime and essential substance, like ambrosia, shared exclusively, but not always responsibly, by Olympian divinities. Though corporations, governments and individuals in positions of authority make decisions that impact millions of lives, their power is concentrated, not dynamic but contained, like the gold in Fort Knox—to be conserved more often than dispensed. Yet despite their strong, pervasive influence in the political realm, corporations wield a fraction of the power in society.

Most of us will never be directly affected by the power of elite networks of politicians and plutocrats, yet we fall into moments of absolute power every day. In each moment, location and situation, we must reckon with the absolute power of others. Such power in varying quantities is allocated to the police officer, administrator, clerk, government factotum, teacher, waiter and mechanic. It is administered to our faces and from miles away by individuals and committees we do not know about and will never meet.

To these characters, and to others who serve and surveil us, we must appeal, not as citizens but as supplicants. Each aspect of our lives is dictated, controlled and modified by that special someone empowered to say yes or no, to act in our behalf or to stand in our path, to make us wait or send us on our way, to move or stand pat, to push our buttons or pull strings for us, to ease our burden or break our backs.

Such moments of absolute power are liberally sprinkled over our lives like salt, to bleed us, cure us and age us. They extend from the perfunctory to the life altering. They include everything from the local cop who stops us for a casual seat belt check to the boss who hires or fires us on a whim, to the teacher or professor who writes a great or tepid recommendation in our behalf. The moment of absolute power frequently passes without incident or reverberations, but it can also crack and explode the moment and scatter debris across our lives. An apparently nondescript event can have lasting impact—the knowledge of this possibility increases our fear and oppression.

When I was a rock and roll singer/songwriter, someone remarked that club booking agents and record company A&R executives were "like gods" to me. I bristled at this analysis of my situation because I was raised as an individualist, and could not abide the thought that I had to prostrate myself to another's will. Yet those who judge our talents rule our destinies.

These satraps stand before the portals of success and failure, emptiness and fulfillment, and hold our livelihoods, our status and our respect in their stern caprice. They wield this control with a high and heavy hand; if they favor us, we move beyond them and they fade behind us. But if we balk and bristle at their power, try to skirt it and deny them their tribute, they can ruin us, or at any rate, spill and drizzle ink on the sketches and blueprints we've drawn of our futures, what we generically call our dreams.

Any job applicant at an interview knows the absolute power of the other. All we have to protect us from the abjection of this circumstance are optimism and faith. The interviewer is an enigmatic tyrant, probing, withholding and taunting the applicant with a hidden agenda. A candidate's future, home and family may be at stake; the interviewer is only doing his job.

Each day is a gauntlet of yeses and noes. When a police officer stops me at a speed trap or a judge is ready to decide whether I am guilty of an infraction, they have absolute power over me within that duration. The policeman can write a ticket or a caution, check my license or search my car. The judge can sentence me to the maximum, minimum, or probation—or declare me innocent, sending me off in perspiring relief and stammering gratitude for having lost no more than a few hours of my day.

While I stand before these figures at the moment when they wield their absolute power over me, I am an extension of their will, just as the steering wheel, computer and wrench are extensions of my hand. Their power controls me remotely and I belong to them. I can resist and challenge their control—which inflames and increases it—or submit to it, accept it for the moment and be released from it under my own recognizance.

The ancient Greeks understood the absolute power of the other in everyday life and its horrific consequences. They embodied it in the sphinx that guarded the gate of Thebes. A monster made of woman, lion, and raptor, the implacable sphinx asked riddles of pedestrians and devoured those who answered incorrectly.

Our one consolation for enduring this intermittent anguish is that the power to which we submit in one moment is history in the next. Once exercised, it is gone—absolutely—unless one provokes and prolongs it. A spotlight fades on the authority and the subject returns to his own custody. I leave the tyrannical moment as a free man—albeit temporarily. One tormenter recedes into the past, as another looms ahead.

Freedom is like sleep—a pause, an emollient, a flight from trauma, as ephemeral and recurrent as subjugation. Freedom is also a pleasure of solitude. As we exit a courtroom, classroom, waiting room, government office, we experience a rush of freedom. It reassures us that prostration may be permanent but not continuous. Yet freedom cannot endure and anyone who mistakes the exhalation of relief and lightness of spirit for a new start, rather than an intermission, will receive a blow when he enters the next absolute power zone. Freedom does not exist on its own but in equipoise with oppression. It can only be measured and appreciated by contrast.

We may believe ourselves solid citizens, but we are magnetic nomads darting between poles of detention and escape. What alternative is there? We can't flee to other climes or within ourselves, pretending power is not real and ubiquitous, or that we have more of it than the society where fate places us.

If we walk away—mistaking delinquency for freedom, skipping bail, as it were—we forfeit our goods, tarnish our name, and sunder the bond held by the one who had absolute power over us. Our true escape comes when power subsides deprived of the resistance that inflames and stimulates it. I once told my daughter that for one term, a teacher had power over her: she would treat her and grade her as she wished. Yet, five years later, I promised that she would not remember what the teacher said or the grade she gave—she might not even recall her name. Power and memory are both unstable.

Memory provides comfort, because of all the living it retains and the misery it deletes. Yet regardless of the tricks memory plays to entertain us, the friction between abjection and freedom will propel us to our next station.

LUCK: THE GOOD, THE BAD AND THE UNKNOWN

Whenever I have been disgusted with life, I have been able to stop the bleeding of second-guessing self-rebukes by asking one question, "Would I want to be someone else?"

Despite all of my mistakes, deficiencies and bad luck, my answer is always, "No way." Backed into a corner of my own making, I come out fighting for my identity, for the life I've made with my own choices—results be damned. I do not want to be, nor can I imagine being, anyone else.

Yet, rarely a day goes by when I don't curse my luck or judgment. I imagine what might have happened if I had attended *that* party, walked down *this* street and not another, uttered a compliment rather than a tactless remark. I ask if boldness or discretion at a key moment might have made a lifelong difference.

But as regret stirs and simmers in me, I turn off the heat. Luck is too detailed and mercurial to change with one stroke. Even in moments retroactively classified as "turning points" how can one calculate the endpoint of an alternative path? Had I acted boldly, I might have been killed or injured. Had I been more discreet in one moment, I might have befriended a secret enemy who would have harmed me in the next one. In a parallel reality, I might look back from the chair I occupy and ask how I got into such a mess over dubious honor and treacherous friends.

The same holds true for the good that did not occur. If I had been a rock star, would I have become an addict or been stranded without steady work and purpose? Would I now be in a haze of faded success that did not sustain middle age but mocked it? Would I envy contemporaries whose careers were extended by a bumper crop of revived popularity, dynamic management and fresh luck?

Luck is invisible and inscrutable, though as palpable as air. We often link it to special occasions, contests or games of chance, but we have no idea how many moments it changes; how often it steers our lives a millimeter to the right or left. We never reckon how many times our luck prevents disasters, how many so-so days might have been our last ones without the intervention of chance. Conversely, we can never know if we would have been better off without the good luck we have received—if we had not won the lottery, overindulged our whims and gone bankrupt.

We hope luck sustains us from moment to moment, that it guides us down the right streets, among the right people and that we never roll the dreaded "snake eyes." Yet there are times when bad luck turns out to be good luck in disguise and we're better off when rejected and denied. We may even be most fortunate when most deprived.

This is no highfalutin version of "sour grapes"—in which a person besmirches a beloved dream. Missing out has often been the best luck a person ever had. Ask Dion DiMucci. The "Teenager in Love" singer was left off a plane to a gig in Moorhead, Minnesota and must have cursed his luck until he learned that Buddy Holly, Richie Valens and the Big Bopper lost their lives on the flight he missed.

Perhaps I have been too demanding. Rather than lament my bad luck, I should ask how much worse it might have been. Only a naïve person believes there is a bottom to bad, while a wise individual appreciates the good breaks he gets when he avoids the invisible bullets flying everywhere.

I admit to being lucky in certain ways. For instance, I have had reasonably good health, have never been seriously injured, and have a close and loving family. On the other hand, I've never won a lottery or any other contest of skill or chance. In matters of luck, I've come out ahead.

Many believe these are idle musings, that "luck is the residue of design" and that we make our good fortune by putting ourselves in the right position to receive it. But going down that path can lead to delusions of grandeur, a self-directed paranoia that says you are responsible for everything, including the laws of probability and chance.

Life has a randomness that cannot be summarily accounted for or dismissed. I can't bear responsibility for what it does and the many arbitrary turns it takes. All I can do is to meet its vicissitudes with all the care and fortitude I have had the good luck to retain.

SELF-HELPLESS

Who Is Qualified to Write a Self-help Piece?

Just as youth is wasted on the young, self-help books are written by the wrong people. Successful individuals and psychologists are way too "together" to tell failures how to succeed. What could they know about screw-ups, bad choices and hopeless situations?

Clinicians see misery and dysfunction from the outside looking in but unless you've made mistakes, suffered consequences and seen your life slip into a permanent loss column, how can you understand the ways that people get stuck or know how to free them? Until you're acquainted with the demons strolling arm in arm with a wretched soul down the stony road of perpetual losing, how can you guide anyone from the brink of oblivion?

I felt a calling to write self-help from the viewpoint of one who has endured painful quandaries. Such a person is best qualified to show you how to avoid or adapt to your own ordeals. Will you hire a guide who studied a strange land or a native who has lived there his entire life?

Ultimately, self-help is the most effective help you will ever get. If you can't solve your own intractable problems and internal dilemmas, how can someone who doesn't know you solve them for you?

Self-help vs. Self-improvement

Self-improvement is an American mania that started with the colonial Puritans and their spiritual diaries. They tried to demonstrate that they triumphed over evil in order to prove they were not eternally damned.

Ben Franklin extended the quest for self-improvement to all people, made it secular and gave it a worldly objective—prosperity and citizenship.

Self-help has always been embedded in our culture, whether it meant improving one's diet, appearance, physical culture, interpersonal relations, self-esteem, sexuality or spirituality. We believe in our power to improve our lives and ourselves.

Our literature reflects this tendency. In his autobiography, Ben Franklin wrote that he "conceiv'd the bold and arduous Project of arriving at moral Perfection" and that he "wish'd to live without committing any Fault at any time." To this end, he devised a list of 13 virtues that he meant to acquire as habits. Much later, in a fictional context, young Jay Gatsby would keep a journal where he, like Franklin, recorded his defects and vowed to rectify them.

For most people, self-help is equivalent to self-improvement. The underlying premise of the genre is that if you improve yourself, you help yourself. This can be true but is often false.

A line must be drawn here between self-improvement and self-help. They are not only different but often opposed. I discovered this discrepancy when I was ten. My fourth grade teacher liked pupils to be quiet and she reinforced this behavior with operant conditioning.

Every Friday she awarded a chocolate bar to the quietest boy and girl for that week. After six months, I had never won a candy bar and I was determined to get one, so I said nothing for a week. On Friday afternoon, I waited for my prize but my mumchance went unnoticed and I didn't win the chocolate. My self-improvement was no help at all.

An influential, if perverse, recent addition to the annals of self-improvement is the film *Groundhog Day,* the premise of which is that an infinite number of do-overs can turn a cynical, narrow-minded jerk into a fine, well-rounded human being. Along with giving new meaning to the idiom "happily ever after," this speculative comedy poses a dark question about self-improvement: what value does it have if we must live several lives to achieve it? If we must be perfect to be good, then self-improvement seems an interminable and thankless enterprise.

Problems in Self-help: A False Start

In the spirit of self-help, I sat with my notebook and pondered my situation. What were my problems? Was I unhappy? Could life be better?

If I thought otherwise, I would be too delusional to write for the self-help genre.

I jotted down a list of things I wanted and didn't have that might improve my life: professional standing; the respect of others; more free time to pursue my interests; the ability to earn a living doing what I do best and love most; a more robust social life; and better leisure outlets than *Law and Order* reruns. At first, this litany of insufficiencies only demotivated me because I had no solutions for them. I slumped into resignation and futility. This was when I realized I was self-helpless.

I tried to live with this prognosis, but I experienced an immediate and sustained resistance against it. When faced with the cold facts of my situation, I could not accept defeat and wallow in self-loathing candor. I had to act, to rise up in defiance of my fatalism in a spontaneous and vital impulse toward self-help.

Self-Eulogy

Julius Caesar wrote that experience is the best teacher. The most reliable source for self-help is personal history, so it makes sense to use the past if we can remember it.

While we experience the present as a sequence of hectic moments that demand rapid processing, not analysis and reflection, history is cured over time. Our blood and sweat are dried and concentrated to flavor our attitudes, while pain and confusion are aged to wisdom and humor.

Before I could learn from the past and devise suitable questions and answers, I had to understand the tumult of my life. At first, this seemed an impossible task for one lifetime. I'd need at least two lives—one in which to muddle through and raise questions, and another in which to answer them. Since I had only one life, writing self-help seemed an impractical endeavor. Still it tempted me. I was too tenacious, compulsive and arrogant to relinquish an impossible challenge. This might be the ultimate self-help question: "How do I let go of a project too big for one lifetime?"

The capacity to distinguish between a feasible objective and an unattainable object is a sign of maturity. Accepting one's mortality is another. I had to allocate my time to projects I might expect to complete. I was about to abandon the idea of writing self-help when I realized that I might complete such a volume in one lifetime, even in one afternoon, if I glossed over every conundrum I had encountered while devising test questions germane to key aspects of my life: work, love, self-preservation.

What difficulties had to be overcome to improve my life? Of the many, a few emerged—inequality of outcome, inequitable distribution of rewards, the randomness of experience, the burden of responsibility, the aggravation caused by others and the struggle to lead a meaningful life.

If experience was the wise teacher, the ideal self was the refractory student in detention. Experience may provide solace, but the ideal self— the composite of all that I wanted to do and to be—was my lifelong tormentor.

Regardless of what we say or do, and what others say and do to us, the ideal self never leaves us. We may try to annihilate it with drugs or alcohol but it clings to us, inspiring or taunting us. It would be better to make peace with the ideal self and let it be the implacable motivator that prods one to faithfully follow the path of a child who never knew where he was going or how to get there but only where he wanted to be.

To achieve this objective, I hearkened back to the most innocent time of my life and summoned to memory the earliest vision I had of my ideal self—untainted by the struggles and disappointments I experienced in my adult efforts to be equal to it.

Then I devised the eulogy test to hold myself accountable to this ideal self of my youth. I jotted down what I wished to be said of me when I died and committed it to memory. Each day I looked in a mirror, recited this encomium to my reflection and asked if what I had done or proposed to do that day was worthy of the man I had wished to become and the memory of me I wished to leave behind.

This may seem a morbid ritual, but it can preserve one's aspirations. We work and love in order to leave behind some part of ourselves, because we wish our lives to be of value to the world and to our descendants. The self-eulogy is an earnest, if crude attempt to define oneself in concrete and candid terms—what we do, what our lives mean to us and may signify to others.

I realized that to feel worthy of the life I am given, I must keep my eulogy in mind and never stray from it. I resolved that while I am alive, I must live each moment with utmost urgency and sincerity since the hands, the mind and the heart of a corpse can do nothing.

The Responsibility Test

I was raised to believe that any bad thing that happened to me was my fault. If a car had struck me while I was crossing a street on red, I would have been blamed for being there at that time. "What were you doing there?" my mother would have demanded. "I was going to the store to buy milk like you told me to," I would have replied. I carried this perpetual, ingrained guilt well into adulthood.

When I was rear-ended on a highway, I blamed myself for driving there at that moment. When I had an interview and didn't get the job, I rehashed the interview and blamed myself for what I said or didn't say, for talking too much or not enough.

Anything that went wrong could have been avoided if only I had done something else, somewhere else, out of trouble. I felt a weight bearing down on me, a psychosomatic effect of the culpability I carried; I was like Atlas Jr. hoisting a world of human sin and error on my narrow shoulders.

Finally I couldn't bear all the blame I brought on myself.

"How is it possible that I'm responsible for everything?" I asked. I threw off the burden of responsibility. It occurred to me that if I had the power to bring so much disaster down on my head, I surely had enough left over to do myself some much belated good.

To stay functional and sane, I abandoned the notion that I was responsible for everything that happened. I resolved only to answer for what I did and how I behaved. What people said and did to me was on them. I realized I could make someone smile or frown but I could not change their dispositions or improve their mentality. Once I drafted this resolution, my mental health improved.

Reward vs. Failure: Do We Ever Really Move On?

Success and failure and how they happen have been at the core of my "American" neurosis. In many religions, and in America, too, success is a sign of divine love. You make it because God loves you more.

In America we assign numinous qualities and implications to success and its trappings—money, power, fame. They signify "being somebody" which is infinitely better than not having these rewards and being "nobody."

Billions of people are thus condemned to a life sentence of voiceless, uncared-for invisibility.

When I was in my 20s and early 30s I often woke up during the night in a sweat with a terrible question in my head, "What if you never live up to what you thought you were? What if you turn out to be mediocre?"

The question was ambiguous and confusing. Was I asking if I was as good as I thought I was, or whether I would be as successful as I wanted to be? Either way, I had no answer for this terrifying query. Hope and faith were my default response.

After years of being plagued by these apocalyptic notions, my wife and I had our daughter. I was nudged away from my youthful ambitions by parenthood. Gradually, those "life-and-death" questions about success were no longer as important.

However, they didn't vanish. They cropped up on Saturday mornings, like old acquaintances, to compare who I was then with the person I had become. After conscientiously driving my daughter to her acting and art classes, I would listen to public radio to stay in touch with the world outside my family only to hear interviews with writers and artists that invariably cast me into despair.

These disconsolate episodes prompted me to ask a vital question that made me duly apprehensive since I knew the answer could determine the quality and meaning of the rest of my life. Is it possible to ever escape the shadow of disappointment?

Dealing With Feelings of Personal Failure

How does one cope with a disappointing career or a career that never was? Or deal with the fact that after choosing a vocation and practicing it your entire life, you can't earn a living from it?

It is remarkable that hard questions can be phrased in so many ways, yet they remain so hard to answer.

A thwarted career is like unrequited love. You never know why it occurs—and you stop analyzing it because it is like touching an open wound and it hurts so much. Over time, what becomes clear is that your calling is only calling you and no one else. You may persevere for a while. There is valor in fighting to the end. Yet a goal that is too difficult to reach might seem a wasteful carnage of emotion, time and effort.

Knowing if and when to quit is a crossroads that defines your life. Even how you phrase and frame the decision is critical. You can issue a public statement to yourself that you haven't failed but have only not succeeded yet, or that you are not renouncing your beloved project, just prioritizing your survival. The words you use may save your face but don't count on them to keep your heart from breaking. Even if quitting is self-preservation, rather than surrender, the pain it inflicts cannot be underestimated.

Some might opine that continuing to work at something when it prevents you from being happy or from engaging in more profitable ventures is a type of addiction. Yet unlike other addictions, the treatment for doing what one loves—even without financial reward—is to keep doing it. To be deprived of a career is agony, but to renounce one's vocation is to survive without purpose, which is barely living at all.

It might seem natural to abandon your life's work when it does not pay the bills, even to denounce it as a waste of time. However, I have found it to be true, and others have confirmed this with their own stories, that by continuing to work at a vocation, even when it has failed to coalesce as a career, you may develop a stronger relationship with your work, do more with it and love it more. Your vocation can become a lifelong friend that will sustain you even in dark times.

How to Respond to Rude Treatment

It is hard enough for us to control ourselves, so how can we possibly control others' behavior?

I always hated it when people were rude to me, when they spoke in an imperious manner or shouted in my face. I thought they behaved this way because they did not respect me enough to treat me with courtesy. I was probably right, but I was still wrong to let their behavior affect me. I took their abuse personally, as if it were a reliable estimate not of their worth, but of mine.

Eventually, I concluded that incivility was our natural state and that courtesy was a perquisite dispensed only when necessary. Meanwhile, loutishness was a luxury only those of privilege could afford. In this perverse worldview, most people chose to be hostile and insulting, and only strivers, seekers and dreamers tried to do better—because they felt they had to.

This was my cynical mistake. Courtesy, kindness and decorum are always virtues, not defects, and incivility is always to be despised. Boors and brutes were to be pitied, not hated. Now when a churl abuses me in order to objectify and demean me, I remind myself that how he treats me reflects how he feels about himself.

Monolithic Thinking vs. Mosaic Thinking

We often approach problems by taking mental shortcuts, believing that we save time by simplifying complex matters. To make ideas and people seem simpler than they are, we group those that seem alike into large units. This is monolithic thinking.

Monolithic thinking is a heuristic that finds likeness in disparate things—and organizes similar items into one category. The larger the class or unit, the more convenient it is and the better we like it. We prefer large headlines, ideas and generalities, and recoil at details and nuances.

Generalities are like closets into which we throw everything in no particular order. They make life seem tidy when it is not. Once we say, "He looks like this or comes from there, therefore he must be like that," we think we know that person and can slip him into the appropriate file or folder. If one thing seems to resemble another, we cry out in delight, "Aha! This=that!" as if we have connected two puzzle pieces and are closer to solving the universe—until *this* is revealed to be nothing like *that*.

Monolithic thinking seems to save time by simplifying the world. It makes us feel smart. The problem is that monolithic thinking does not produce true understanding. It gives us false confidence in our viewpoints until we realize we're mistaken. Monolithic thinking yields spurious information and prevents us from acquiring valid knowledge we can use.

Mosaic thinking is an alternative to monolithic thinking that eschews simplicity and compels us to perceive the complexity of most things. Mosaic thinking starts from the premise that each thing is different until proven otherwise, and should be viewed as such. Mosaic thinking tells us that each situation must be evaluated on its own terms—even if it means learning new terms.

Is There Life Beyond Our Goals?

Birth is a dream; death is a fact; life is the puzzle in between.

Each of us has a destiny. Some might call it a "shelf life." We do what we can until we can't. Most of us think we have only one gift to share, one talent. This skill becomes as intrinsic to us and how we present ourselves as our names and faces. When we can no longer do it, or are deprived of the opportunity, we believe we have nothing else to give.

Others can adapt, self-modify and assume new roles. These brave chameleons explore their identities, develop latent aptitudes, learn skills and establish new goals. This response to change is a gift that encompasses self-awareness, mental agility, the courage to relinquish what is precious and to seek what is new, and the imagination to see more possibilities in life and for oneself.

Franz Liszt was an audacious artist who embraced change. He was an anomaly in his time and still stands as a model for self-invention and self-expansion. Liszt was a musical prodigy who stopped touring when his father died. Inconsolable, he taught music until, inspired by Paganini, he returned to the concert stage and became the first superstar pianist. After years of inciting "Lisztomania" with his virtuosity, Liszt switched from performance to composition. Later, after two of his children died, he renounced music to become a priest.

Each of Liszt's incarnations was enriched by those that preceded it and all were imbued with intense spirituality and unstinting integrity. Liszt was unafraid of relinquishing his spectacular musical gifts because he knew instinctively that they were the means to an end, not the end itself.

Special abilities are portals through which individuals find freedom and fulfillment. They can also be prisons where people forget the difference between who they are and what they do. Individuals confined by their capacities and accomplishments are like Norma Desmond, the deranged silent film star in *Sunset Boulevard*. They cease to adapt and function, but rather sequester themselves in their own cerebral museums.

We are taught to strive toward a goal and not to quit until we reach it. It would be wiser to see beyond our goals and discover in ourselves the same depth and diversity we observe around us. Just because we climb a mountain doesn't mean we have to live on the summit.

The Laundry Room Oracle

I have an embarrassing admission to make. I have never been good at taking advice. Moreover, I despise self-help books. I tried to read *The Power of Positive Thinking* and got depressed. I read some chapters of *How to Make Friends and Influence People* and got into a fight.

One person, however, almost got through to me with sound advice at a pivotal moment in my life. She was a woman I met when I was 22, during the summer between my year abroad and my life in New York.

Diotima cleaned apartments in my mother's building. I met her while I was doing my wash. We struck up a conversation that turned to the meaning of life and how to lead a good one. Despite or perhaps due to her many strivings and setbacks, Diotima believed herself an expert on life.

As we chatted between the spin cycle and the drier, Diotima shook her head with a rueful smile. I asked her what was on her mind. "Nothing," she lied. I knew she wanted to tell me something significant and I took the bait. "Tell me," I insisted. "It's nothing," she demurred.

Diotima remained reticent but her eyes were gravid and judgmental. I coaxed her to deliver her oracular insight and admonished her that it was wrong to tease me. She said she withheld what she thought because I might not be ready to hear it and she didn't want to harm or offend me. I argued that I was over 21 and of legal age to hear anything. This persuaded her.

"You must surrender the things you want most and the life you wish for yourself," Diotima intoned in a low voice. "If you do, you will find happiness and truth. Maybe not truth, but happiness. But if you don't do this, you may never be happy."

Diotima must have guessed from my gloomy face that her wise edict disappointed me, so she waved her hand and added, "It's best to do what you want. You will learn for yourself."

I liked her second directive better than the first and followed my own inclinations. In the end, Diotima's perceptions were accurate, but renunciation was beyond me then because it surpassed my level of maturity. Still, I had no regrets. Starting out mature is like reaching a destination without a journey.

Does Self-Help Really Work?

The best self-help is to cut yourself some slack while the surest way to improve is to look in a mirror each day and ask, "What am I doing here?"

Self-help is paradoxically the most effective assistance because we're the only ones who can help ourselves. If we can't figure out what we need and what makes us happy, no one can.

I once believed people focused on details because they were afraid to face a big picture. Now I ask, "What's wrong with that?" Attending to small things like hygiene, food and a clean home can keep one sane and content.

When we are unable to solve, understand or even think about major problems, apparently trifling details may give us sanctuary from our intractable concerns. They can absorb our attention and provide subjects to focus on and master until we regain our equilibrium, confidence and strength to cope with seemingly overwhelming issues.

Discouraging quandaries don't vanish. They hover until they eclipse everything. We need a balance of large and small concerns and to fill our days in the same way that we fill a jar of rocks and sand: big items go in first before we fill the spaces between and around them with granular details.

The Best Self Help? Help Yourself—To More Life

Life is the sculptor. It creates us with relentless pounding and destruction until we find the form hidden within us.

I acknowledge that I rarely ever conceived, planned and carried out a self-improvement. Most good things in my life have come by happenstance and evolved over time, or stopped abruptly with limited effect.

I see myself now and how I was at 20. I am unchanged in my core aptitudes and traits. Maybe consistency and immutability are individual triumphs and the capacity to be loyal to oneself in strength and weakness is a benchmark of emotional health.

One way I learned to improve my life was to enjoy it more. It wasn't a matter of beautifying my environment, visiting fine places or taking drugs to make oil drums and power lines look like natural wonders. I had to make an internal adjustment, to appreciate what I was doing and where I was, and to savor each moment on its own terms. Life is heaven if you look at it the right way and remind yourself, "I'm alive and I could be dead."

This tough love enabled me to dilate. For once, I enjoyed waiting at the supermarket checkout behind a woman with ten pounds of bacon and four six packs of toilet paper. I celebrated standing for an hour in a packed train stuck in a tunnel while inhaling fellow commuters' halitosis. I rejoiced in heavy traffic and opened the windows to imbibe the exhaust fumes of idling trucks. I believed that life was bountiful.

Your eyes roll and you shake your head. You don't believe scrubbing toilets or waiting in a smelly basement for an elevator to come will ever make anyone's "bucket list." You surmise that I've washed my brain with a useful fiction or chosen stupidity to protect my sanity.

However, it may also be true that delusion like truth can serve a higher purpose. Our intellects convince us there is always somewhere more beautiful than where we are and something more interesting and significant to do than what we are doing now. Intelligence makes us feel we are equal to our aspirations and better than our circumstances—all of which makes us unhappy.

If you subscribe to monolithic thinking and apply the same standard to everyone in the belief that there is just one way to succeed and be happy, you will become like matter sucked into a black hole—crushed to a single point and absorbed by the greater mass. How much better it would be to adopt mosaic thinking and acknowledge that no two people or situations are the same. Then success, failure, happiness and melancholy are yours alone, without comparison, since they are intrinsically different and unique.

Anyone can analyze your dreams, but no one can fall asleep for you. Waking to the splendors of living comes individually, like a parcel on your doorstep. Will you sign for it, remove the gift from its box and put it to use? The hardest part of receiving a gift is learning what to do with it, but that is what we are here to do. When we help ourselves and heed our own advice, we start to make our way back from the brink of oblivion up a steep path to the fulfillment of our lives.

HANGING ON AND LETTING GO

Nothing is at last sacred but the integrity of our own mind.
—Ralph Waldo Emerson, "Self-Reliance"

Persistence is not a uniquely American virtue, but like many virtues in the world, Americans have bought a controlling share and made it our own. American history is relatively short but it demonstrates repeatedly the value of tenacity in the face of mortality, suffering and despair. Our core belief is that all failures are roads to success; if you "hang in there" long enough, you can win in the end. It is the Gospel of Optimism.

"Hang in there!" is a seductive idiom. It puts hypothetical limits on any ordeal and makes salvation sound imminent. "Hang in there!" suggests that help is on the way. Yet this is more sanguine than accurate. You may have to *hang in* far longer than you imagined. Reinforcements may never arrive and your tribulations may never end. Conversely, optimism is an attributional style that can raise our morale. It can encourage us to take risks and extend ourselves in ways that may bring fulfillment if they do not kill us first.

Hanging in is easier with social support—a person or group to *hang out* with it. If you have no one to talk to, you might be tempted to invent a companion, as Tom Hanks did in *Cast Away*, when he turned a volleyball into a best friend. Social support is not a given and it can come at a steep price. People who share your convictions do not magically appear, while others with aspirations of their own may compete with yours. We are too idiosyncratic and diverse to harmonize without effort or compromise. When we modify our plans and ultimately our goals to accommodate others, it becomes clear that tenacity is a virtue that abjures social intercourse. *Hanging in* is often a solitary affair.

We must go alone. Isolation must precede true society.
—Ralph Waldo Emerson, "Self-Reliance"

For social people, *hanging in* can pose insurmountable problems.

Gregarious individuals abhor being alone and can easily sacrifice personal freedom for social acceptance. Alexis De Tocqueville noted that despite the American cultural bent toward individual freedom, Americans are susceptible to groupthink and often submit to the tyranny of the majority. This phenomenon has not changed; social media and a 24/7 news cycle have only exacerbated it.

Yet, transcendental thinkers proposed an antidote to the hell that is other people: *self-reliance.*

Self-reliance is not self-love but a survival manual. It acknowledges that we must provide for our physical and spiritual needs, and defend ourselves if necessary against all manners of attack by individuals and institutions. Self-reliance demands that we be attuned to our environments. It tells us that all things in and around us are related and we are stronger for interacting with them. It also warns us to keep an accurate account of ourselves at all times.

For me, self-reliance sprang from the realization that what I wanted most in life I could not get from others but only from myself. This was a crucial insight but a painful one, since I was a gregarious soul who enjoyed and sought out the company and approval of others. For many years, I defined myself by what others thought of me and struggled with seclusion. The only way I persevered through the difficult adjustment from sociability to solitude was by assuring myself that my solitary activity was a pathway back to society and the acknowledgement of others.

When I started to dedicate myself to writing and taught English to support myself, I vacillated between writing a novel, which would consume enormous time and effort, demand solitude and sacrifice, and might go unpublished and unread, and dashing off art reviews, which were easy work and gratified me with publication and readership. I knew art reviews were ephemeral and soon forgotten and that I should devote myself to creative projects. Yet I was addicted to the fast and facile reward of often seeing my name in print and could not resist it. I knew I was cheating myself and was conflicted by compromise. I lost self-respect and despised my weakness for balking from my life's work.

My reckoning came while I taught English as a Second Language on Saturdays at a community college. My supervisor was a Ph.D. candidate in sociology. We became friends and I related to him my dilemma. He admonished me to do what artists had always done—to go off somewhere, unplug from society, work in obscurity and wait to be discovered.

> *These are the voices which we hear in solitude, but they grow faint and inaudible as we enter into the world.*
> —Ralph Waldo Emerson, "Self-Reliance"

It was difficult to hear what sounded like a prison sentence but I knew my colleague was right. My choice was clear—between present sacrifice or lifelong regret. I needed to tear myself away from parties, by-lines and the social life I always depended upon if I was wished to achieve my goals. If I balked at this, I knew my life would be a disappointment to me.

I fully imagined the stark deprivation that lay ahead. By undertaking this challenge, I would need to rely on myself for inspiration and motivation. I dreaded the enormity of what I was giving up. This self-reliant way of life was bearable only if viewed as a transient adversity, a rite of passage to be rewarded later. I envisioned one day being invited back to the social life I had forsworn and receiving the fanfare and admiration of the world that had lost track of me.

With such happy thoughts of redemption in my head, I worked and struggled with reclusion. I completed projects and submitted them but none led me back in triumph to the society I sorely missed and craved. The world was oblivious to my offerings and I had to rationalize this outcome. Was it the indifference that welcomed novelty or was I not good enough? I chose to believe the former and persisted in the scalding rain of self-doubt.

It soon became apparent that this seclusion in my own personal wilderness was no probationary period or training camp to be endured for a specific duration, nor the harsh anteroom to a cozy and familiar parlor. It was an all-encompassing way of life. There was no guarantee that I would ever be discovered and validated. I felt like a forsaken soldier on a forgotten atoll in the middle of a soundless sea.

Each day, I peered out on the invisible horizon of my romantic expectations for signs that this isolation would end. I greeted the stirring of every hope as a harbinger of my imminent discovery by others and the warm embrace of society. The fulfillment of my boyhood dream to be celebrated and admired suffused me. But nothing happened. These moments of hope were at last buried under a multitude of years.

I finally recognized that if I defined solitude and self-reliance as means to an end, and viewed my discovery as an event others created for me, I would never be fulfilled. Only when I relinquished childhood dreams and lost hope of being found would the solitude and self-reliance I needed to achieve my goals be more than trials and tribulations—they would be their own rewards. Only then would I become the person I wished to be.

Even when I made peace with my relative seclusion, it was never paradise. I still dwelled in a city apartment ensconced in noise, congestion, inconveniences and intrusions. I had jobs, paid taxes and woke up each morning to the elephantine screech of a garbage truck as my reveille. I discovered that self-reliance came with fine print. It was no panacea. To the contrary, it often betrayed the objectives it was meant to promote. It aimed for freedom but could entrap the spirit.

Self-reliance requires self-defense and presupposes evidence-based accountability. It can no longer stand on a foundation of faith. It must be buttressed by documents, keepsakes, receipts and vestiges of the past. An archive of personal papers must always be accessible since at any time we may need to vouch for who we are, where we've been and what we've done.

This is the business of life and we must tend to it or risk our freedom and our chance for fulfillment. Self-reliance compels us to be ready for any challenge to our autonomy and integrity. We are warned to save tax returns, court judgments, jury summonses, warranties, service agreements and insurance forms. Once retained, these records must be managed and accessed. Self-reliance is thus fortified by discipline but cluttered with papers. The only respite in this endless cycle of details is the nervous hiatus between windowed envelopes that threaten our security and peace of mind.

At times, I confront this trap of self-reliance. Recently, I searched for instructions to relearn how to preset a radio channel. In the process, I excavated a trove of obsolete manuals for appliances I no longer own. Another folder was stuffed with contracts for cell phones I had not used for years.

I jettisoned these files and temporarily experienced the lightness of *letting go*. But this purge only freed one drawer among several file cabinets. Many others remained glutted with articles on a variety of passing interests, drafts of writings short and long, even itineraries and participant lists for meetings I attended years ago.

In the spirit of *hanging in*, I filed these documents in the belief that if I disposed of them, I might one day need information only they contained. I also "hung on" to ticket stubs and toll receipts to prove my whereabouts if I should ever come under random suspicion for crimes committed at those times. Self-reliance may degenerate into paranoia.

Self-reliance protects identity, which depends on history. History explains and legitimates the present in terms of the past. I clutch tokens of my experience because they remind me of where I've been and what I've done. Otherwise, how do I know my life unfolded as I believe it did, or that it happened at all? Without relics of my past, can I be sure that I am not a fictitious character or a profile created by a human resources professional?

Hanging on to relics and memories of the past can defend against the erosion of time and filter out the noise that bombards the mind. Recollection often musters action and focuses thought, yet it has a downside. I keep multiple drafts of my writings to protect against plagiarism. This is a practical measure, yet what purpose is served by filing rejection letters? *Hanging on*, in this instance, no longer reflects selective judgment but an indiscriminate reflex. Demoralizing details of the past can be scars on the psyche that record damage suffered and recovered from and leave invisible markers along the silent path of time.

Why drag about this monstrous corpse of memory...
—Ralph Waldo Emerson, "Self-Reliance"

Freedom can be defined in part by our ability to know who we are, what we've done, perceived and understood. By the same token, self-reliance ensures the integrity of our impressions. While I am *hanging in*, I *hang on* to memories and objects as evidence of my experiences and insights, as well as my capacity to continue to have them.

Meanwhile, habits and routines give form to the lonely tenacity of those of us who self-reliantly *hang in*—working and living in obscurity. Our time is unaccounted for and may appear to depreciate, when the opposite is true. Habit and routine give structure to time that otherwise passes unremarkably. Without external support—friends and a broader social circle—habit and routine can lift one's spirit and imbue life with a unique character. It can also distinguish one day from another.

When does self-reliance devolve into petty control of a diminishing world spent in perpetual isolation? Does hanging on to my original ideals prevent me from experiencing freedom? Surely, my life must be more than a fortress defending its sovereignty against its own insignificance. I must *let go*.

By *letting go* I do not mean reinvention, a popular theme in American culture. Reinvention is our materialist form of reincarnation, in which identities may undergo as many changes as can be squeezed into a lifetime. Reinvention can be an existential escape hatch from a dead-end identity, arousal from a nightmare, or a spiritual version of bankruptcy in which one is released from moral debt and permitted to restart clean as someone else.

Hanging on to as much as you think you need is one form of self-reliance, but *letting go* of many things because you don't need them is a better one. I knew a vice president and executive creative director who always came to work without a briefcase. With free hands and shoulders and an easy gait, he looked more like a juvenile delinquent showing up late to school than a top-flight executive. One morning we entered the building together and took an elevator to our floor. There I was with my leather shoulder bag, so prepared and professional, and I remarked half-jokingly that the creative director, my boss many times removed, never carried a thing. He smiled with enigmatic mischief and pointed to his temple. "It's all up here," he said.

At the time, I believed he was indulging his eccentricity, which he could afford to do. It only occurred to me later that he was a paragon of *letting go*, demonstrating what it meant to be truly self-reliant. In an industry where image was everything and instability and impermanence were norms, he had freed himself from things, and felt sufficient and secure without props, papers, meeting expectations or winning approval.

Letting go is no escape, but an acceptance. It is neither surrender, nor resistance, but independence. If I *let go*, I will not walk off, give up or give in, but take a middle path, meeting society's demands while I explore my reasons for being. Discipline will be my guide, but never my master— without it I am lost, yet I won't be ruled by it.

The alchemy of imagination can distill a thousand failures into one success, but *hanging on* with faith and persistence can provide the strength to carry on and move forward. Yet defiance and tenacity cannot deliver promises or grant wishes. To have the fulfillment I seek, the burden of self-sufficiency and sacrifice must occasionally be lifted. In their place, I must have the confidence and freedom to *let go*.

Letting go is no euphemism for going slack and inattentive. I continue to *hang on*, to stay vigilant and make sacrifices, with one eye always open. But as I defend the fortress of my wishes and convictions, I see beyond its walls and venture forth. Even slaves in the Bible were given manumission in the seventh year. I hold on to my dreams but set them free to pursue them. In my relentless and weary striving, I may yet become the self I envisioned and find personal truths where they always were—locked in my emotional safe box. When I can refresh my persistence and resistance with self-expression, I realize the person I wished to be is who I am—and the world I hoped to discover me is where I am—it's the one I created.

A TESTAMENT TO JOURNAL WRITING

The underlying concept of keeping a journal is that writing has a utility that can benefit a writer apart from its impact on another reader. We believe that putting words on a page or screen is a public performance that demands formality and expect our verbal expressions to be judged by others. Otherwise, what would be the point of making them?

Creative and commercial writing put a premium on basic competency and typographical perfection. Neatness counts and how the writing appears can signify more to the reader than its content. Spelling and grammar are mandatory criteria one must meet to be taken seriously.

However, journal writing spins the act and craft of writing in the opposite direction. It stresses the private and the personal value of self-expression. Journal writing is deliberately unguided and unformatted. It is not meant to be judged or even seen by others. When you write in a journal, it doesn't matter how the words look on the page, if the punctuation is perfect or whether sentences are between the lines. It doesn't even matter if you write sentences.

By providing a private, personal dimension for self-expression, a safe "reader-free" zone where words exist for their own sake, journals free writers from the constraint of trying "to get it right the first time." Creativity is no longer on the time clock, facing deadlines and editorial scowls. It is a form of play, what Claude Levi-Strauss called *bricolage*— methodical chaos. Insulated from standards, markets and critical eyes, journal writing broadens and redefines self-expression.

We often view rhetoric—the use of language to persuade—as a device to assert ourselves and our ideas, even to impose our will on others. Writing in this context is an instrument—or a weapon—to obtain power. However, journal writing is *laissez-faire*—you possess your work and control it. You are a creator, editor, critic or none of the above. In this sense, a journal is the space where you as a writer are free to encounter what you think without the interference of the others out there or inside your head. There is no reason to wonder, care or know about anyone else's opinion of your journal. There are no submission requirements.

The writing one does in a journal is not a hard and tyrannical skill to be scrutinized and judged by others, but a creative exercise with therapeutic value. A journal is a laboratory where ideas are dissected like cadavers or a sketchpad where inchoate notions are adumbrated and defined. Journaling may provide an alternative channel for the thought or experience of a moment when an hour cannot be spared. It can also be a spillway to protect "serious" projects from extraneous preoccupations and distorting emotions. Above all, a journal is a friend—intimate, personal, without monetary value and supremely trustworthy. It can belong to no one but you.

Journal writing can also improve one's attitude toward writing. It can be the mental equivalent of yoga or meditation. It permits and encourages one to write freely, which can have a broader impact on creativity. For self-expression to be honest and effective, it must be free and relaxed. Yet our creative norm is often cramped and inhibited because time and effort are so excruciatingly precious that when we write, we feel compelled to make every word and moment count. We may strain so hard to choose the right word and to do too much with it that we freeze and fumble. Journal writing segregates expression from constraint.

I first learned about journal writing at a university workshop for composition instructors. My attitude toward the subject could be euphemistically characterized as skeptical. If I had not been paid to attend this workshop I doubt I would have been there. I was too proud of my writing skills and achievements to believe that I ought to squander them on private and personal communications. I felt that writing had to "count," have a purpose and objective and that my time was better spent on work others would see. Journal writing seemed an insult to my proficiency.

The leader, an unassuming educator from Vermont, explained to the workshop participants how useful and liberating a journal could be. He claimed that it was an all-purpose book, where we might jot down ideas, everyday stuff that happened to us, rough drafts—whatever we wished—without self-editing or concern about the writing quality.

Our journaling guru proposed a litany of benefits to journal writing. He assured us that it would help us overcome our compulsion to be perfect the first time. This alone would make us more effective writers, by reinforcing writing as a process, rather than a nervous feat. He delineated less obvious advantages, as well. Keeping a journal could improve our memory and mental hygiene by sorting the clutter in our minds and putting it to use, or by removing it altogether. It might also arouse the first impulses that inspired us to write, the fun of moving a pen or pencil across a page. On these private pages, we could be self-indulgent and silly—doodle, draw cartoons or embellish our letters like medieval monks.

By the end of the workshop, we neophytes were expected to embrace journal writing in our lives. Still I remained a doubter and a naysayer. I saw scribbling in a notebook as a frivolous waste of precious time. I swore I was too busy writing novels, stories, essays, lectures, articles and poems, while teaching a full course load, to fit into my life the kind of journal this evangelist advocated. I scoffed at "free writing" as the literary equivalent of free love.

I continued to resist journal writing, although I was aware of its uses and benefits. I knew, for instance, that the psychotherapist Ira Progoff had used journals as a therapeutic device to help people access their unconscious. It was also true that I had kept a diary for years, though it was neither therapeutic nor expressive. The leather-covered books I received as gifts each New Year were daily agendas. Each day had its own page like a two-dimensional office for the mind. Anything that happened on a given day was noted in a sentence or paragraph, and everything, including my commentary, had to fit on a page. Since I forgot to report each day's activities promptly, I often had to go back and retrace my days, filling in one or two weeks of undocumented time in one fell swoop. It was a struggle to differentiate one day of the recent past from another and I filled in blank pages with snippets as if the diary were a puzzle. Days were often represented by a few words like "Rain all day," "Wrote 10 pages," or "Interview, 10 AM." I kept such quasi-diaries for years but never a journal.

Gradually I added emotional content to the dry record of my days and my diary became more than a skeletal account. I wrote how I felt about the experiences I noted: my discomfort at the job interview, a particularly good tuna sandwich I made, the heat of the laundry room and the dryer that left the towels damp. I started to fill the pages. Gradually, the 1-page per 1-day constraint frustrated me. I bought leather-covered journals without day and date headers, so that one day of activities, emotional responses and ideas could flow onto multiple pages.

In time, I resorted to two journals—one served as a daily diary, the other as a real free-form notebook. The former remained a record of my days, while the latter served as a record of my mind. The journal became an indispensable tool. It did not impede or distract from serious writing, but facilitated it. In a journal, I trapped random ideas that came to me while I was immersed in other things. Later I might insert these ideas if they were germane to my formal writing.

Journals are of greatest value as mental filters. Often, thoughts and feelings I experience in the course of a day can find their way into my work, whether they belong in it or not. In a creative fury, I may believe I can make new sensations and impressions fit in my current project, but they often clutter and distort it. By writing passing ideas and feelings in a journal, I can keep ephemera at a safe distance from works-in-progress.

Storage is the only downside to journal writing. Since journals document one's work—and life—I want to keep them in reach. Over time, they pile up and compete for shelf-space with towels and clothing.

If our creative acts are extensions of our lives, exoskeletal scaffolds that protect the frail vessels of our bodies, or gorgeous responses to irritation like the pearls oysters make, then journals are worth the space they occupy in your life and on your shelf. They are nothing less than the contents of your mind as they come to life and wend their way to the surface of consciousness. There they may inspire immediate development or lie dormant, gestating until the next wave carries them forward.

163

THE INVISIBLE BLUE INK

It may seem fairly obvious that the content and style of our work reflect our personalities and experiences. What we may be less aware of is that even our methods link us to remote locations in our psyche that we rarely visit, which we inherited not only from vague recollections of youth, but from ancestors we never knew we had.

I have kept a journal for many years. The numerous volumes of this work occupy a long shelf in our supply closet among guest towels and surplus toiletries. They are an odd assortment of untitled books—sleek leatherette English diaries, marble composition books that cheer my inner child, spiral notebooks with clear plastic covers and coiled metallic spines that get entangled, and brightly colored notebooks that ad agencies give to new employees as desk-warming gifts.

Even publishers of mass-market paperbacks would agree that you can't judge a book by its cover, yet my collection of journals belies this proverb. To the contrary, the outer appearance of each of these chronicles speaks volumes about me biographically and chronologically—what I was doing at specific times, how much discretionary income I had and how I felt about journal writing at the moment when I obtained them.

Whenever I wish to locate a specific event from a year, month or date in the past, I can dip into these journals, refresh myself in memories and take solace from the fact that I remain anchored in a coherent swatch of time, a work in progress titled "My Life."

But I made a troubling discovery just the other day. I was trying to recall the details of an event that took place in 2015, so I went to the linen closet, pulled the 2015 leatherette journal from the shelf and opened it. To my dismay, the blue ink on the page where I sought my answer had badly faded. Then I flipped through the journal and found that almost all of the pages were equally faint and illegible. It was as if all of 2015 were disappearing before my eyes in a thin gruel of watery ink consumed by thirsty paper.

It was no mistake that I wrote my journal in a lighter colored ink with a cartridge pen rather than with a darker ink and a bolder implement. I had learned early on in the sedentary journey of journal writing that dark ink and a bold nib make a lasting impression on two sides of a page, rendering the obverse side unusable. Washable blue ink appears gentler, easier on the paper and the eye. Yet even sound practices can go awry.

I continued to pore over the 2015 journal in shock and disbelief at my bad luck. As I assessed the damage, I considered what I should do about it. This faded tome demanded a major restoration but I had limited time. I could not justify rewriting a personal document whose contents I did not expect to share with anyone. What difference did it make that many of its pages were illegible? A journal contains the arcane trivia from my life that even my closest kin would be disinclined or unable to read.

On the other hand, letting the words of the journal fade into oblivion undermined the purpose and effort in writing it. 2015 was not utterly uneventful and beneath memory; I resolved that it should not become the frangible stuff of oral history. I would retrace my steps through that year by tracing over a few hundred pages of pale and eccentric handwriting.

Having never aspired to be this generation's Samuel Pepys, I did not relish this unforeseen chore. As I laid coats of ink with my scratchy nib on the badly faded characters, I groaned at how many pages I had to restore and how long each one might take. As a year, 2015 was neither bad enough to erase, nor good enough to relive, but it surely did not merit so many hours of the current year to commemorate. I found myself hating those times all over again as I re-read anecdotes about a tedious job, an abusive boss and a chandelier that crashed on our dining table while we sipped coffee on a Saturday morning. Retracing the journal of 2015 gave new meaning to what I'd heard old-timers say about their lives, "I don't want to go through that again!"

At first, I performed my restoration only in the margins of the day, when I was too tired for more productive tasks. However, I felt like a fool for giving it any time at all. I rationed my effort. I went through the book and traced only the "key words" on a page that seemed most important, but this was a risible half-measure. One word in the middle of a sentence is like one letter in a word—it only calls attention to what is missing.

As I devoted more effort to the restoration project, it expanded beyond its original scope. My commitment intensified. I was on a quest not just to restore the record of a year but to honor memory, itself, preserve the past and uphold the value of personal writing.

Every day, I pored over the journal to assess my progress. Regardless of how many pages I had saved, there were always many more to reclaim. Such is the thankless nature of restoration. There are no shortcuts, only long detours; the more you do, the more work you have. As the number of legible dark blue inked pages increased, they made the faded pages around them look shabby and the days and incidents they depicted seem less important.

Restoration often entails destruction. By bolding the characters on one side of a page I made the good writing on the obverse side illegible. I had no alternative but to retrace every page, even those that had been faded but readable. As the project grew and the work compounded, I felt miserable and out of control, albeit helpless to stop myself. Compulsion is the dark side of dedication. I quickly and all too easily became "consumed" by this apparently boundless and thankless task.

During scraps of time, a half-hour borrowed from now and then, I stooped over my journal, meticulously retracing faded blue lines and circles of whimsical penmanship. I could feel my back curl and tighten. My eyes strained and my vision blurred.

"What are you doing?" my wife asked.

"Nothing," I said half-truthfully to conceal my painstaking time-wasting from her. But when I failed to come to dinner she investigated.

"Honey, why are you rewriting your diary?" she asked with genuine concern and gentle amusement as she regarded my rigid torso hunched over the faded pages. "I understand that you're fascinated, perhaps even obsessed, with the past. But is it necessary to trace over everything you've already written so that you can confirm that you ate a hamburger on such a day or opened a new pack of underwear two, rather than three, years ago?"

She asked fair questions and made valid points. I felt like a dolt but I couldn't help myself from being one. I was driven by a force I could neither stop nor identify. It wasn't simply that I was hung up on the past—the details of 2015 were patently worth forgetting—but that part of me remained in it, my footprint.

Gradually, I took artistic liberties with the characters I restored, filling in the cracks between the ghost lines and the bold veins of retracing. "Now you're truly wasting time," I reproved myself. "You just want a hobby." It was not far-fetched because I had briefly taken up calligraphy years before. Now, after tracing the letters of a page and augmenting them with volume and shape, I appraised the result of my effort and exhaled with satisfaction. The page resembled an ancient parchment with the sumptuous characters of a Hebrew text, a version of the Bible, perhaps, or *siddur*, a Jewish book of prayer.

What began as a mission to save 2015 from obscurity had led me in an unforeseen direction. I was expressing an artistic tendency of which I had been unaware. Had my childhood years in Hebrew school made such an indelible impression on me that I recapitulated those lessons years later? Or was I fulfilling a need so deeply ingrained that I had no clue that it existed until the disappearing ink triggered its release?

It occurred to me that I was behaving like an ancient scribe, summoning from the depths of unconscious memory the professional scribbler that my distant ancestors might have been. I remembered the Egyptian sculpture *The Seated Scribe* I had admired in the Louvre. Maybe he, or someone like him, was my Greatest Grandfather.

Yet, it would be inaccurate to characterize this diary restoration project as a New Age spiritual act to "channel" a scribe ancestor. Such a mystical spin would be irrelevant here since the influence of this forebear must have been entombed in my psyche for eons, waiting patiently for his cue to be reborn. Even so, this was how gifts frequently revealed themselves: something outside summoned what was within, like a childhood friend asking me to come out and play.

Retracing my faded diary no longer seemed to me an inexplicable tic, but a birthright. The blood of scribes flowed in my veins and from my pen onto the faded letters. All writers can claim this pedigree. Without it, I would have renounced this glorious and wretched vocation years ago. The impulse that compelled me to restore this journal for hours at a time might have also induced me to continue writing despite innumerable discouragements.

By restoring the text of my faded journal with more elaborate lettering, I retraced atavistic proclivities that had gone dormant and apparently withered like a Rose of Jericho, the resurrection plant, only to return to life at the first opportunity. These attributes once predisposed someone to be a scribe—fine motor skills, patience, an inner silence that sealed out extraneous sound, a focus that filtered light, an ability to translate speech into phrases on a page, an eye for chirography's abstract design and a satisfaction at bringing meaning to an empty page.

When writing was new, such proclivities and aptitudes would have been all that a scribe required. The purpose of writing then was not to convey individual thoughts, emotions and activities as I often do, but to document on parchment, stone or clay what people said, who they were and what they bought, sold, demanded and expected. (Only later would religious texts be added to their repertoire). Ironically, the skills and components of the scribe's trade were aspects of writing most people now value least. (Only 21 states require cursive writing to be taught in school). Yet I found myself updating the scribe's ancient art to slavishly fulfill my need to keep intact a residue of my quotidian past.

As I flipped through the retraced pages, I particularly admired the thick, sensuous curve of the S and the round knobs I had fashioned on both ends of the "f." The world today has no use for such filigree. Today writing does not produce a thing to look at and admire. It does not bear the mark of the individual hand or the soul of the maker. Twitter sums up the current view of what writing ought to be—a quick statement to convey a message or a caption to a picture, if possible. The appearance of the characters and how the words are spelled are irrelevant.

It wasn't always this way. We no longer admire writing but our ancestors doubtless venerated it as a transformative act. The FOXP2 gene involved in speech and language achieved its modern sequence 200,000 years ago, the *Blombos* cave engravings were done 100,000-130,000 years later, and written language made its first appearance in ancient Sumer 5,500 years ago. When our ancestors made the last leap to writing—after thousands of years of discussion—it must have seemed magical. The ability to communicate and understand one another made society possible, while preserving thoughts, beliefs and transactions on rock, slate or clay gave strength to law and permanence to culture.

Today, we may view writing as an inconvenient and imprecise way to convey ideas, but for the early practitioners and readers of written language, the characters on parchment were intrinsic to the power of the words they embodied. In holy texts, the characters contained the aura of the scribe and the divinity that inspired him.

Not that I would ever claim to be a scribe incarnate. I know I am a technologically assisted writer who types symbols instead of drawing them, uses his fingertips rather than a full hand, and inscribes words on digital stationery, not papyrus. Yet due to a self-inflicted chore prompted by disappearing blue ink, I happened upon the primitive and discarded core of writing.

This discovery of an ancient aptitude in myself was not unprecedented. The phenomenon has been expounded on in two intriguing, though not scientifically proven, theories. According to biologist Rupert Sheldrake's concept of *morphic resonance*, non-genetic "fields of information" enable life forms as diverse as termites, orchids and pigeons to transmit their knowledge to future generations.

Through *morphic resonance*, individuals inherit a collective memory from ancestors of their species. *Morphic resonance* may account for how certain birds migrate thousands of miles and arrive at the same place, and for why most English speakers in a study distinguished between gibberish and a Turkish rhyme without knowing a word of Turkish. *Morphic resonance* may also explain the human tendency to express the traits, skills and proclivities of ancestors without being aware of them.

Meanwhile, Carl Gustav Jung's concept of *collective unconscious* maintains that we carry in the unconscious libraries in our minds an archive of symbols, ideals and even landscapes. These figures are derived from the origins of society and culture and have become a deeply rooted and broadly shared system of "patterns of instinctual behavior." According to Jung, these "archetypes" do not appear in a linear, regional or homogenous manner for a European might dream of an Aztec god.

While Sheldrake inferred that Jung's collective unconscious was evidence of *morphic resonance,* the Swiss psychiatrist was not alive to comment on their compatibility. Hence, the link between these two theories remains speculative. However, what is clear is that retracing the invisible blue ink of my 2015 journal with fresh, bold veins of color bound me to the traits, skills and aesthetics of my ancient ancestor, the scribe. It also clarified that putting words on paper was the tip of a deeper vocation.

"If the past is pressed up…against the present," as Sheldrake mused, I wondered how many of my tendencies were ancient heirlooms? As a Jew, my affinity for dry places, like New Mexico, North Africa and Southern California might refer to my unconscious yearning for the Middle East. But I don't need a desert to sense within me the presence of my ancestors. I am most deeply related to them by my penchant for chronicling my life. Retracing the faded characters of my 2015 journal recaptured two levels of my past—my immediate existence and the distant lives of scribes who transcribed the mythology, history and ritual of *their* ancestors.

Does this personal discovery have a broader relevance or therapeutic value? Retracing old words may seem like a form of writer's block, though I was not procrastinating but restoring an irreplaceable item. To the contrary, I discovered that this project might be a remedy for writer's block. Retracing my faded back pages did not inspire the writing of new ones. Yet it induced a meditative state during which pressures abated and putting words on a page ceased to be a cerebral test or a supernal art. Rather, it revealed itself to be a manual craft that produced concrete and satisfying results.

In the end, I salvaged the events of 2015 from the voiceless depths of unrecorded memory and placed the journal on the shelf with the volumes that came before it. In the process of retracing the many pages of faintly visible blue ink, I was able to recall moments I'd forgotten and to relive others I wished to suppress. I realized that 2015 was a year full of activity and emotion—and a diverting detour from the present.

As I revived the words and memories of 2015, I excavated an artifact from a deeper past, an obscure and hitherto unknown love of ancient handwritten characters. This is no doubt the script in which the operating system of my soul is written. The scribe in me remains alive after many millennia. The mind loses nothing. It merely misplaces objects. And what keeps the longest in our gray jelly is how we do things, not only the style of our words and deeds, but our methodology—the pattern of our thought and action.

Process is personal: how we do things reveals more about us than what we do. It was not a revelation I expected to receive from writing. I often consider the content of my life in terms of what I do and think about, and the choices I make. Yet the means and tactics I employ are also intrinsic to who I am, the messages I send and the projects I undertake. I learned more about myself by how I restored my 2015 journal than by its contents. Writing has many functions, one of which is self-discovery. If you wish your writing to tell you more about yourself, don't just stare at what you put on the page but rather think about how you put it there.

THE POSTMAN ALWAYS THINKS TWICE

Earlier today, our longtime postman was leaning against the mailbox outside the building, waiting for a truck to dump the pile of mail he would deliver. With his elbows pressed against the mailbox dome and his chin inches above its cold metal surface, our conscientious mail carrier struck a sculptural pose of human superfluity and mythic suffering. After 30 years of toiling for the postal service, he was treated as an afterthought who was reduced to waiting around to do his job.

"I'll write a play about you," I promised. "Waiting for the mail."

He smiled. "Like waiting for Go-*dot*, right?—Oh, I'm dating myself."

"Relax. You're not dating yourself by knowing about *Waiting for Godot*. It's one of the most influential plays of the mid-20th century. It epitomized the Theater of the Absurd and depicted a world without certainty, meaning and God. You could have read it in high school anytime in the past half-century."

He nodded, blinked and stared down the road as if praying for the mail truck to appear. "Really? That's great. Thanks."

"No problem," I replied as I walked off to move my car from one side of the street to the other so I could move it back 90 minutes later.

But there *was* a problem. I mulled over the implications of what the postman had said. He believed he sounded old because he recognized a reference to the most famous play of Nobel-laureate Samuel Beckett. Was it shameful to know such information?

I understood the unease he felt. Referring to any person or event from more than five or ten years before often felt like you were admitting you worshipped Satan to the Inquisition.

I had even violated my own know-it-all principles by holding back before making certain references in public. I avoided alluding to history altogether—even the Vietnam War sounded way too "back in the day." To mention "Woodstock," "transcendental meditation," "acid rock," "peace demonstrations," "the bombing of Cambodia," *Easy Rider*, "civil rights," or even to use the term "disco" pegged me as old, if not senile, or as having taken the wrong college courses.

When I taught English literature to remedial students, a colleague archly pointed out that we wasted our time teaching John Donne's "The Sun Rising" and Andrew Marvell's "To His Coy Mistress."

"My students think the Civil War was America's war of independence. They think World War II happened 150 years ago. They think Mary Queen of Scots owns the company that makes toilet paper," he declared at an English department meeting.

Senior faculty shuddered at his mordant observations. They loved Metaphysical poets, believed everyone should feel the same way and it was the teacher's fault if they didn't. They wrote off my iconoclastic colleague as a defeatist and did not rehire him. Senior faculty continued to teach Milton—one professor literally with his eyes closed—to undergraduates who had last opened a newspaper to house-train their puppies.

(Did I just mention *newspapers*? I date myself.)

Not long ago, back in the pre-digital dark ages, it wasn't cool *not* to know things. Ignorance was neither blissful nor hip; to the contrary, it prompted eye-rolling disrespect. Most people put a high value on cultural literacy. It was okay to identify music that wasn't on the Top 40 (just dated myself again), and to visit a museum and know what you were seeing. Those days are gone. Now most people rarely if ever visit a museum, read a book, a magazine, or even a tabloid (now also nearly archaic: a paper dominated by provocative headlines, large photographs and captions.)

"Dumbing down" is now like "keeping it real." The more you know about the world and how it got this way, the less people want to hear from you. Your references go right over them and they shake their heads at your irrelevance. It's the revenge of ignorance: it condemns erudition as old, geekish, out of touch and as funky as an old bookstore. People conclude that if you know about the Hundred Years War, you must have fought in it.

Computers and associated technologies were purported to be the foundation of the Information Age. It is amazing that you can Google-fish for facts and snare them in seconds. Yet the only information many of us seem to care about pertains to technology, itself—when the next Apple gadget is rolling out, what it will do and how well it will perform. The knowledge people prize most is about the latest app, the latest film, and the latest episode of the latest hot TV show: if it's not the latest, it's too late.

The celebration of now and the empowerment of ignorance are apparently two tines of a multi-pronged conspiracy to keep most people running in place, as they consume the latest ephemeral item produced to create a life-long loyal consumer base. Rather than cultivating a widely knowledgeable citizenry, our schools and media have raised a human herd with no mentality for other times, cultures and values.

One proverb states that if you don't know where you came from, you won't know where you're going. But what happens if no one cares where we're going—if the only concern is going and getting there—somewhere, anywhere?

Another classic epigram warns that if we don't know history we'll be doomed to repeat it. If this is true, then today's consumers are impervious to doom because we repeat our actions, buy the same devices, see films and their sequels multiple times, and watch reruns of the same TV programs ad infinitum with no qualms or irony.

Beatniks were legendary for saying on any Friday night, "Let's drive to Cleveland."

"What's in Cleveland?"

"Does it matter? Let's just go."

To a boy of fifteen, the Beats' spontaneous absurdity and freedom made sense. However, Kerouac, Cassidy and their restive cronies were joyriders rolling against a conformist tide, whereas today's unmoored "just do it" crowd are carried by it. Their undirected restlessness is often tethered to a routine as they escape through their eyes to another space. Will they know where they came from or where they're going when the tide rolls out? Will they even know where they are?

SOMETHING NEW ON A SULTRY AFTERNOON

I heard a shocking statement on the radio, which is not surprising since shocking statements are the defibrillator paddles that keep radio alive. A sports talk host remarked that there are so many sequels and remakes in films and television because there are no original ideas left.

This declaration was most outrageous due to its hypocrisy. A sports radio personality who decries the lack of original thought in our culture is like a heavy smoker denouncing air pollution. Yet despite my issues with the messenger, the shock jock's message was hard to repudiate. Given the many sequels and remakes today, one wonders if creative people have stopped trying, if the audience has stopped thinking—or both.

We welcome minute improvements to our gadgets, yet return like domesticated pets to the same superheroes and storylines we've enjoyed for decades. Will we be satisfied to stay pat with our mythology in perpetuity, pouring old wine into new flasks until we're swilling vinegar?

Here a distinction must be made. There is no dearth of original ideas; they are just not produced for mass consumption. Decision-makers in the entertainment industries do not wish to test new ideas in a marketplace where Tried and True are superheroes.

Originality falls into a vicious cycle: a new idea cannot be popular if it is not expressed; but if an idea is not already popular, disseminating it is an investment no one will make. Novelty is voiced in the wilderness.

This schism between originality and accessibility in the entertainment media is a phenomenon I encounter daily.

As a writer, I spend many hours in a quiet room. For company, or accompaniment, I listen to musical CDs. While I can rely on the quality and diversity of my selection, changing CDs is inconvenient and breaks the flow of my work. I must sometimes resort to entertainment from another source, so I tune into the TV and radio.

This cultural dependency forces me into a paradox: despite a plethora of stations and networks, there is so much of the same thing across every platform. Each station or network plays the same content repeatedly and today's films, songs and television programs are very much like what was presented five and ten years ago. Even shows I avoided in my youth are now broadcast years later, as if to give me a second chance at what I didn't want before.

Repetition is intrinsic to routine and routine is the metronome of discipline, which is integral to a good life. Routine is as necessary as a steady heartbeat and deep breathing. It enables efficiency and security—even relaxation. Yet too much repetition can do insidious harm. If you perform the same tasks in the same place, week in and week out, and fill your leisure time with the same music, programs and films, you don't need to dig a grave, because you're already in it.

This is what happened to me. My work was going well but when I got tired and tried to relax, I found nothing novel or interesting to entertain me. I seemed to be sequestered on a small island, ringed by a sea of boredom.

But then one humid summer day, I turned on WKCR-FM, the Columbia University radio station, and heard a voice I'd never heard before. It was strong and hoarse with a round, exuberant warmth, like a honking horn, singing soulful, eclectic songs. I listened with pleasure to these fresh, infectious sounds, and was eager to know the identity of this artist who was so different from anyone I'd listened to before.

Van Ronk's music has been around for years, but for me it was a belated revelation. Van Ronk played old time jazz songs with brio on his acoustic guitar and sang with the relaxed power of a blues man. His cover of bluesman Blind Blake's song, "That'll Never Happen No More," about a man who had a series of disastrous encounters with shady women, was so joyful and *immediate* that I was shocked to learn that Dave Van Ronk had died 15 years before. It seemed a travesty that I discovered him so late, but I could also see it as more inspirational evidence that a thing well done is done forever.

Soon after Van Ronk, another great and original voice came on the air. It belonged to Mississippi John Hurt, whose calm, elegant blues singing and infectious guitar work have a soaring quality in inverse proportion to their subtlety and quietude. The biography of Mississippi John came to mind, how he appeared on the blues scene many years ago and tried to get a recording contract and a tour, but was overlooked and denied the chance to further his career. John Hurt returned home, gave up music and did menial labor. Decades later, a musicologist discovered a track Mississippi John had recorded and hunted down the legend until he found him in a shack. The great bluesman no longer owned a guitar but when he was handed one, he played it like he had never stopped. As I listened to the hypnotic, elegiac recording, I reflected sadly on all the music John Hurt might have made that we would never hear, because his talent went unrecognized for so long. Yet I was grateful, too, that he was not altogether silenced by preterition.

That sultry afternoon, a world usually cluttered by remakes and retreads showered unforeseen beauty and originality on my existence.

Hearing Van Ronk and John Hurt in sequence might have been too rich for my soul. I burned up this stimulating stuff and fell into a state I call *spiritual hypoglycemia*—for lack of a more clinical term: too much sweetness followed by dearth and depletion. I was lethargic and needed a pick-me-up, so I pulled over to a Starbucks and waited for the counterperson to brew a batch of fresh coffee. Just then, as if I had not received enough brilliant new content to last me as long as a crocodile's supper, I had my third musical revelation of the afternoon.

It was a song from a different era with a sound at once familiar, yet fresh enough to make me wonder who was making such cool, invigorating music. "You're right as rain," the soulful tenor's voice intoned as backup singers harmonized behind him. This tune that was new to my ears reminded me of "It's Gonna Take a Miracle," which I had heard many times before. Yet this record was just different enough to make me forget the more familiar one and I became rapidly entranced in what I was hearing now. The ensemble sang with a blend of doo-wop and vintage soul. I remembered the hook, "You're right as rain" and looked up the song on my phone. These were *The Stylistics*, a group out of 1970s Philadelphia.

The Stylistics sounded familiar to me, and I might have heard this group's music many times without knowing it was theirs. The song stuck with me and I hummed it all the way home. Some soul songs are like that—they go with the summer like lemonade. I researched *The Stylistics* and "You're Right As Rain." Thom Bell and Linda Creed, both in the Songwriter's Hall of Fame, composed this song and other *Stylistics* hits. Tragically, Linda Creed was diagnosed with breast cancer at the age of 26, though she wrote songs until she died in 1992, at the age of 37. Now the work of this American original was coming to me decades after her untimely passing.

On that Saturday afternoon, I experienced a repletion typically reserved for primal experiences like a rich dinner or a restful sleep. But this was far better because it reassured me that there is always enough original talent to sustain us for the foreseeable future.

When I drove cross-country, I divided states by whether I passed through them by day or by night. I saw the day states in detail (Nevada, Nebraska), while the night states (Indiana, Ohio) I barely saw at all. The same simple taxonomy may apply to artists and their work. They are original and extraordinary but until I experience them by day, I will doubtless miss them at night.

I read all I could find about the artists I'd just discovered. When I encounter something I admire, I study it to preserve my impressions of it. I did this as a child and I hope that if I continue the practice, it will keep me young. The fountain of youth is in the mind; the secret to immortality is to do our best until our strength fails.

That sultry afternoon I learned that a dirge for original ideas is premature. When artists die, their originality endures for years beyond, perpetually renewing itself—even when ignored or overlooked—because no one and nothing can replace them. You don't need to trek far and wide to appreciate something new and different. It can be anywhere and come from anyone, dead or alive, and it doesn't matter how long it's been there, because it's fresh when you find it. Times change, we change, but fine, original work never gets old and it never dies.

ACCEPT YOURSELF

There is a time in every man's education when he arrives at
the conviction that envy is ignorance; that imitation is
suicide; that he must take himself for better, for worse, as his
portion...
            —Ralph Waldo Emerson, "Self-Reliance"

Acceptance is often thought to be a consolation prize in the sweepstakes of life. No one aspires to this feedback, yet our psyches crave it. We strive to be respected, admired, loved or feared—in our dreams, perhaps even adored. These are high-stakes, high-status responses that thrill us for a moment, engorge our egos and puff our pride. Yet they cannot comfort or sustain us. Only acceptance does that.

We won't find acceptance at an office or on a dais. Acceptance is not a career goal or a word to be wished for in a recommendation letter. In our occupations and jobs, we can neither hope nor aim for acceptance because it is not a valid endorsement in the public and professional spheres. Even if it were, we wouldn't want it.

When we offer goods and services, only our work is germane. Those with whom we interact are not involved with who we are, only with what we do. Customers don't want to *accept* what we sell them—they want to *love* it. Typically we pay for satisfaction, excitement—or even fulfillment if we're very demanding. Acceptance is a shrug. It has no place in the market.

Yet, because it seems so homespun and anodyne, acceptance is one response untainted by money. It may be earned but it is never paid for. Like parental love, it is freely given. It is a reaction that presupposes a detailed familiarity with one's defects. It incorporates effort, resolve, compromise—and commitment.

Self-acceptance often sounds soft, self-indulgent and complacent. We satirically associate it with schools that give awards to children for competing, not winning, or with the couch potato who gapes at sports while gorging on empty calories. On the other hand, acceptance is such a strong internal force that we are drawn to people who accept themselves. We say of these blessed few that they are "comfortable in their skin."

Acceptance is mundane and underestimated, yet it has a profound impact. It is also mistaken for other responses.

Though acceptance is often based on appreciation, they are different. Appreciation anticipates and embraces the good, whereas acceptance suspends expectations and concedes the presence of frailty. When you are accepted, you are fully accounted for—your merits lauded, your flaws forgiven.

Appreciation is a spotlight that beams on you alone, whereas acceptance points in two directions—at a specific individual and at life in general—and applies one set of values to both. When people accept you, they reveal an attitude not just toward you but toward all things.

The love one feels for another may include acceptance. Yet acceptance differs from love and friendship, which may come and go *without* acceptance—while acceptance is constant.

Admiration, appreciation and respect are public responses to the public-facing individual, but acceptance is intimate, wise and all embracing. It means knowing someone and still caring because of or in spite of what you know.

In this sense, acceptance is a stronger bond than marriage. It signifies that someone of sound mind has chosen to take all of you after knowing what you have said and done when you were unscripted and uncensored.

Acceptance is also a lasting peace that ensues after conflict and confusion have passed—when people know no further adjustment can be made and things are as they are. It is a gift we rarely receive.

We are transparent to those who accept us, so we never feel ashamed in their company. Any discomfort at their impending judgment dissolves like an old argument.

Yet the acceptance of those who know me best cannot soothe or heal me if I don't accept myself. I seek clemency from my harshest judge—his black robe is my own skin. The acceptance I need most only I can give, by acknowledging who I truly am in all of my strengths, deficits, hopes and disappointments.

Those who brook my weakness deserve my sympathy. Those who know and love me pay a price—but I pay a higher one.

This is why self-acceptance is so difficult and so essential.

Self-acceptance would seem to come naturally. According to a romantic view of existence, we fell from an idyllic state of self-acceptance at the moment our parents expected us to develop "normally"—to walk, speak and use a toilet. They compared our progress with that of other toddlers and anxiety crept into their loving gazes. Instinctively, we knew we had to do what they expected to hold their affection.

Later we were thrust into classrooms, where we were forced to compete with peers for attention and approval, and to confront our strengths and deficits. The seeds of self-rejection were planted there and started to sprout.

We are looking-glass-selves to a point—from an early age we are shaped by others' opinions. Yet certain people seem immune to feedback. They accept themselves innately. Is it genetic? Is it a flood of one hormone or the dearth of another, or it is another form of intelligence entirely?

I could never accept myself. I only saw who I was through the prism of my dreams. Self-acceptance would have required self-awareness, which I believed would crush me.

When I entered school I always vied for teachers' favor. I compared myself with rivals and tried to mimic or outdo their attributes. If such adaptations exceeded my mimetic skill, I was tormented by the deficits I could not eliminate or rectify.

These fault lines in self-acceptance spread and deepened. Some related to school—I wanted to be better in quantifiable subjects like math. Others were physical details. I looked in a mirror and wished I had blue eyes and straight, thick hair rather than the briar on my head that I combed and tugged at to no avail. I disapproved of my thin body and wished to be thicker, faster and more muscular.

Fortunately, my survival instincts would kick in. I laid aside my self-objections and found qualities worth liking, promoting, utilizing and improving. Yet still lurking under my veneer of confidence were weaknesses I never accepted. The demands I made for self-acceptance were unconditional and stern. I could never accept myself as anyone but the person I wished to be.

When I became an adult, the talents I took for granted no longer worked. I drove myself to earn the approval of others and my own acceptance—and received neither. People shut me out. I blamed them but also myself. I wished I could do things I couldn't do and be a person I couldn't be. I even hated writing, the core of my existence and identity.

I berated myself for falling short and misspending my life. I wondered if things I might have done or said or restrained myself from saying and doing might have made a difference. My blunders baffled me.

I spoke and gestured like a puppet of my obsessions, lashing out at others, though my conflicts were internal. Then stricken by remorse, I sympathized with anyone who cared about me.

I tried to push aside regret and suppress my failure but their ghosts lingered inside me like squatters. I was a self-castigating prisoner of unmet expectations and festering disappointments.

Self-evaluation is healthy, self-improvement depends on it, but it can be the enemy of self-acceptance. Like an immune system run amok, self-evaluation can destroy everything in its righteous path. By blaming myself for all that went wrong, I harmed the bad and good in me indiscriminately.

Between dejection and rage, I found no comfort. People advised me to change occupations so that I might lead a more peaceful life but I scoffed at their counsel. I countered that a new career was like a fresh bandage on an open wound. Instinctively, I felt that cosmetic touches would be not benefit me and that I could only heal through self-acceptance. Yet this seemed tantamount to surrender, an admission of defeat. Anyway, what positive difference could it make?

It would have made all the difference. Even a recluse who shuts out the world must live with himself—and what is living worth if you are in perpetual torment and your universe is a cage?

Sometimes I questioned whether my mistakes were mistakes at all, since my character and background had predisposed me to make them. Were my actions as natural to me as other traits like my height or color?

However, these rare moments of reprieve were transitory and quickly superseded by agitation and pain. I needed to accept myself but I could not bring myself to do it. Acceptance was a reward I believed I did not deserve. I had no compassion for my suffering. I drove myself harder in order to persist and prevail.

Then came a reckoning. I realized that unless I accepted myself I'd never do my best or become the man I wished to be. As long as I looked in a mirror and always saw the enemy, I'd battle with myself until there was nothing left of me.

In this moment of clarity, the slow process of self-acceptance began.

I didn't miraculously start accepting myself. I still blamed myself for too much and carried too much regret. I was so conditioned by misery that even my happiness was infected by mistrust. To be self-accepting after a lifetime of self-censure, I needed to think in a new way.

Many people hope for Heaven or reincarnation. They believe this existence is one phase of a longer cycle. However, the predominant philosophy of our culture can be summed up by the Roman proverb, "Seize the day and place no trust in tomorrow."

Yet while "carpe diem" can inspire boldness, it is also anathema to self-acceptance. The belief that this is the only life we have can make us impatient and desperate, as our time seems to slip away. We believe our faults and confusions restrain us and waste our vision and vitality.

If we were sure of reincarnation, we could take comfort that we had more lives to play with and be patient with our mistakes. But if death is the endpoint, we are raring to make the most of the time we have. When we stumble, we kick ourselves like mules wishing to be thoroughbreds. We know each moment is urgent and what we fail to do now will be our loss for eternity.

The Puritan ethic only ratchets up the pressure. It admonishes us that good luck comes from God, but bad luck is our own fault. What goes wrong we ought to improve, and when things go right, we must still do better.

Feeling responsible for what we are, what we become, and for every moment in between omits chance and circumstance from our destinies. We forget that we choose the cards, but we don't shuffle the deck.

To believe that the full freight of our lives falls on our shoulders is masochistic hubris. The ancient Greeks astutely envisioned the fates as three goddesses that weave our lives before shearing them from the loom. We make our clothes but we don't spin the thread.

This is not to say that we must accept fate, with no freedom to change. We can improve—but not without self-acceptance.

Self-acceptance is often mistaken for self-satisfaction—uncritical contentment. But the two are as different as a hug and a rowdy cheer. Self-satisfaction says, "All I do is right and every outcome is good!"—whereas self-acceptance spurns outcomes. Regardless of how a person feels about his results, he accepts himself if he approves of what he has done.

Just as meditation is more than closing one's eyes, self-acceptance is more than telling the face in the mirror, "I accept you." At times, our true selves are not disguised by deceit but by false reproaches and a selective memory for outcomes, rather than the full story of how they came to be.

You may blame yourself for everything because you believe guilt is easy or that it makes you sympathetic. But assuming undeserved guilt makes you a scapegoat, not a hero. It may be useful to others, but it won't help you accept yourself.

Ultimately, trust is the key to self-acceptance: you must believe your perceptions are accurate, that your thinking is clear, and that you've made the most of the information and opportunity you've received.

Memory helped me re-establish this trust. If I reflected on key moments in my past and re-enacted situations I experienced, I was able to reconstruct what I thought and felt at the time. As time passes, such details are ordinarily forgotten or rearranged, so I needed to restore them to be my own witness and confirm the choices I made. When I was able to identify with the person I had been, I could make peace with him today.

Eventually I accepted myself, but I can't say how or when it happened. It wasn't an epiphany, nor has it been final and permanent. It is more of a truce than a lasting peace. I got tired of fighting with myself.

My attitude changed. I no longer cared too much about my wants, needs and place in the world. Something my mother once said now made sense: See your goals as important, but insignificant. Or put another way: be serious, but don't take *yourself* seriously.

Now I shift in and out of self-acceptance, with occasional flare-ups of chronic self-loathing that come when I'm off-guard. I let them run their course. At least I know what they are, and can cope with and contain them.

Lately I've been upbeat about my life. Since positive feelings normally come to me as often as a solar eclipse, I wonder what's wrong and try to understand them. How did self-acceptance come to me without "life-changing" events?

Three possibilities present: 1. My life is more interesting now; 2. I've become interested in many things that once bored me; 3. I appreciate life on its own terms.

The latter has the most promising implications. Instinctively, it makes sense that by accepting life, I accept myself. Ultimately, life-acceptance and self-acceptance merge into one because life is not something *out there*, like a daunting mountain, a dance partner or a wrestling adversary. It is in me and I am living it.

MY PREMATURE OBITUARY

I recently received a highly unusual friend request. It read, "I stumbled across your name. I had heard that you passed away in the 1970s. It is so great that you did not. I always admired your intellect..."

The message was too stunning and personal to be spam, so I accepted the request.

A friend from secondary school had contacted me unexpectedly. He and I were always the skinny guys in gym and were matched to wrestle each other when we "studied" this virile, sweaty sport. I hated being forced to wrestle my friend. He was a gentle soul and the only boy thinner than I was. Even so, I had to try to beat him because we occupied the lowest weight class and I couldn't bear the shame of losing and the shibboleth as the weakest boy. I proved my manhood by grabbing, throwing, holding and trying to pin my friend to a mat, while he tried to do the same to me. The violent ordeal lasted a few minutes. When it was over no one cared about the outcome. The other boys thought it was a funny sideshow. We were both still the weakest boys in the class.

As I re-read my old friend's message several times, many emotions churned in me—relief being the primary one. I saw myself briefly through his mind—as someone who was revived, restored, reclaimed from the dead. But then after I pondered that I had been believed deceased for decades, I had to imagine my life story in a radically different way, as a much shorter existence than the one I knew.

It was satisfying to exceed expectations, rather than disappoint them. I tried to imagine the reverse scenario—how a person would feel if he tried to reach someone he believed to be alive only to learn that he had died.

I knew what that was like. I once hand-delivered a postcard to someone who was a great friend of mine in the past but whom I had not seen in years. She had helped me launch my musical projects long ago before our careers and lives diverged. Now, decades later, I was scheduled to read an excerpt of my rock and roll novel on a radio broadcast and I wanted to share this event with her, since she had done so much to make it happen. I made a special trip to her apartment building and asked the doorman to give my friend the postcard announcing the radio program. He gave me a long look, as if I had rapidly transformed from just another stranger to his least favorite person.

"She passed away last year. From cancer."

How terrible and guilty I felt! What I had intended as a tribute to my old friend translated as bumbling disrespect. While I demonstrated that I remembered her, I called greater attention to how much I had neglected her. Fortunately, my secondary school friend was spared the same futility and loss because he had found me alive.

Being resurrected without knowing it felt unexpectedly good, like an object might feel when redeemed at a lost and found. Second chances and comebacks are wonderful and rare occurrences, the true four leaf clovers of life. I often imagined that I would make a comeback—to the person I always strived to be. However, in the category of comebacks, returning from the dead must be the main event.

Learning that I had been given up for dead made me feel like a mythic figure, but I was not the first or most dramatic individual to ever be thought prematurely dead. In *The Adventures of Tom Sawyer*, Tom spectates his funeral and hears himself wept about and eulogized as he hides in the church. But while this is just one comic episode in a novel teeming with improbable incidents, Luigi Pirandello wrote an entire novel about the phenomenon of being dead and alive.

In *The Late Mattia Pascal*, the protagonist, Mattia, an indolent ne'er-do-well, reads his obituary in his local newspaper while he is on a train. He has been misidentified as a man who drowned in a millpond. Rather than return home to clarify this misunderstanding, Mattia exploits it. He travels to Monte Carlo, wins a bundle and keeps pretending to be dead.

Complications ensue. In 19th century Italy, it was apparently as illegal to impersonate a corpse as it was a police officer. However, Mattia Pascal's legal problems are minimal compared with his emotional and practical ones. He realizes he can never create a sufficiently robust fictitious identity and background to lead a second life. Nor can he go to the police if he is the victim of a crime. He must always live outside the world of records, where each life is accounted for and his own is stricken from the list of the living. Mattia concedes that his situation is untenable. He has a "George Bailey" moment, "dies" again, this time as his alias, and returns to his hometown to reveal that his obituary was a hoax. It turns out that the joke is on him. Life has gone on without him: his best friend is now happily married to his "widow" and they have a child together. Nonetheless, Mattia finds peace as he resumes his life.

Naturally, significant differences exist between Mattia Pascal's mistaken obituary and my own. His name was wrongly and *conveniently* attributed to a corpse, because his wife, mother-in-law and acquaintances had little use for him anyway, and he went along with the ruse to start over and undo his muddled and insignificant life. In effect, he conducted an informal thought-experiment. For my part, I never attempted to conceal that I was alive. Far from it: I did everything short of advertising on billboards, swimming a circle around New York, or standing in Times Square in a *Speedo*, to call attention to my life status. The federal, state and city departments of taxation all know that I live and where to find me.

Literary precedents aside, it was good to know that someone who had known me so many lives ago was glad I was still around. I had clearly made a good impression in my personal prehistory, the time that had ebbed beyond my recollection. His brief note conveyed two principal messages—that he remembered the best in me and had retrieved me from hell. It may not speak well of my usual perspective, but his affirmative response to my unexpected survival made me feel better about my life.

This should not be misconstrued. I am not depressive or suicidal, and I am glad not to be dead; I'm just not happy enough about being alive. I have my reasons for falling short in enthusiasm, which you may or may not share. Being alive is not often lively or fun. Each day seems to dole out a helping of stress, injustice, inconvenience and peril. Predators are everywhere. Creditors devour me like piranhas while multiple layers of government slice me like *ikizukuri,* a living sashimi.

Nor is it only my own middling life that teeters on the precipice. The news is perpetually dreadful. So many global threats abound that I have been looking forward to the remote possibility of immigrating to other planets. Each day I am twisted and torn by worries about those I care about: are they healthy, happy and secure? Nothing is certain, everything is at risk. Regardless of how simply I try to live, life knots itself spitefully like an old phone cord. Given my usual grim attitude, hearing someone from my past tell me how glad he was that I was alive reminded me to be happy about the fact, as well.

It was oddly fitting that I had not thought about my friend for many years, yet I accepted his Facebook friend request without hesitation. When I read his name and message, his thin, pale face with horned rim glasses returned like a slide on a carousel. His was the immortality of a good soul.

Yet while I gladly returned to life for his sake, I soon brooded over an unsettling idea. He joyfully rediscovered the living me because someone had misinformed him that I was dead. Why would anyone circulate this morbid rumor without confirming it as fact, unless they wished it to be true? Someone from my early years must have wanted me dead so badly that they couldn't wait to read the obituary.

This lifeline from the past also raised disturbing implications. My friend and many others had believed me dead for 40 years, and that long expanse of time now assumed a different shape and meaning to me. I considered the heaping helping of life I'd received since my presumed passing. I reviewed my existence as if it were a newsreel, then snipped off most of it and tried to imagine that none of those years and moments ever happened. But the thought-experiment wouldn't work.

The closest I could come to it was to mourn the major events and vivid memories of joy, passion, activity and life that would not have occurred if my long-lost friend's information had been accurate. Those 40 years of experiences, banal to others, no doubt, but of singular charm to me, now felt fortuitous, even stolen, like an accounting error made in my favor by the Department of Fate. My life might have been a 40-year loan: had I defaulted on my borrowed time or paid it off in full? Did I have anything left? Was my old friend's joyous discovery of my lost-and-found life an ironic portent of a final ending?

The recognition that I had been dead on a distant grapevine then infected my morbid mind with the power of suggestion. I wondered what it would be like to be dead. I re-read passages of the St. Ignatius Loyola's *Spiritual Exercises*, in which the first Jesuit tried to prepare the reader for death by prescribing meditation, prayer and some quiet time in a coffin. To achieve a similar effect without going through the effort and expense of buying a coffin, I lay with my eyes closed on the floor of my dark bedroom and solemnly contemplated my imaginary corpse and a party of lugubrious mourners. In this manner, I intended to confront life's transience and the permanence of the soul.

In my dark speculative mood, I wondered if my secondary school friend's serendipitous message was from another world, informing me that the time I had led since my presumed time of death was *lagniappe*. Now I could put my affairs in order and face the real death that awaited me in the near future, knowing that my life had not been cut off tragically early, but rather, that death had come for me mercifully late.

After these morose interpretations had lost their novelty, the strange tidings had a much different effect on me. Knowing I had been taken for dead made me feel like a jackpot winner. I realized that I had discovered a treasure trove of time overflowing with lifelong experiences and events. I had not been cheated of a second. The swindled ones were the gravediggers who scrawled my epitaph on lavatory stalls and wrote me off in the most extreme and devious manner. I scoffed at my doomsayers. How disappointed they would be when they learned that I defied their wishes by living and thriving. Their malediction uplifted me.

The suggestion that my life might have been snuffed decades ago then washed over me with wonder and gratitude. The presumption of death was like truffle dust sprinkled on my existence. My life finally felt like the precious gift greeting cards said it was and not the daily deadlocks and ceasefires I often experienced. I realized I should savor each day I was given. Nor was I the sole beneficiary of this communiqué. I had unintentionally made another person happy by merely breathing. Not a bad day's work. Mistakes sometimes work in your favor.

It may have been a coincidence that I woke up recently with the thought, "I don't know what death is." In the past, this would have ruined my day with morose anxiety as I mused on the horrid mystery of it all. Yet on this recent morning, I stated my ignorance of death as a blunt, ordinary fact. I was as clueless as the next person about what it means not to be. And that was okay.

But now this text message from an old friend provided new insight about what being dead might mean.

One life is not exclusive to one narrative, but comprises parallel lives with multiple storylines. The other existences unknown to me co-exist in the minds and hearts of other people. For some, I am dead, while for others I am alive. For souls who have not seen me for years, my youth will be etched in stone, yet for those who see me on a daily basis, I am as old as time. My life is not one line. I lead as many parallel lives as the number of people who think of me. Each one tells a different story and has a different feeling about me.

My old friend's message underscored another facet of being dead—one no longer exists for others except as a memory. Yet in this instance, I continued to exist in two parallel universes—dead and alive. Perhaps I had stumbled on a clue about a more complex metaphysical reality in which a person might cease to exist in one life, yet persist in another. If death were not an endpoint on a flat line segment, but one point among many, scattered like billiards across multiple dimensions—and who could verify that it wasn't?—the grim reaper might be just one character in one episode among a cast of millions in a series of infinite episodes. It was a baffling possibility.

Rather than feel crushed and confused by realizing I had died in many people's minds many years before, I rejoiced in this glitch because it offered a simple demonstration of immortality by eliminating the finality of death. For my friend, I had been remembered in death only to be welcomed back to life. Cryogenics was as cold as ice by contrast to this elegant twist of fate.

However, my premature obituary does not end on a grace note, though I wish it did. How great would it be if such adventitious news could be smoothly processed as a macabre anecdote to share over a beer?

I had given considerable thought to my friend's message about my fictitious death and all of its implications, and I believed I had come to terms with it. However, this prognosis was as premature as my obituary.

The incident did not dissipate and dissolve into the ether of memory and random social media. It seeped into my unconscious and I awakened in the middle of several successive nights with a peculiar feeling in the gray zone between sign and symptom, where the lines between mind and body are indistinctly drawn.

As I take a labored breath and feel a suspicious twinge in my arm, I reflect on how many years I was supposed to be dead, and I wonder if my friend's message was an omen that my real end time is at hand.

I cry out silently, "I'm not ready to die. I have so much left to do. My family needs me!"

Suddenly, I have the uneasy sensation that I *am* on borrowed time and a voice deep inside confirms in a low voice, *"All time is borrowed."*

I plead for my life to an unseen and implacable force, when just days before I marveled at how vigorous I was and how great I felt.

Unable to sleep, I turn on the television low and drift off while watching a war documentary. Knowledge is power, but I would have taken blissful ignorance in a heartbeat not to be walking in the shadow of my premature death.

BIRTHDAY REBORN

In our family our daughter's birthday has always been a special day. From her first birthday through her primary and secondary school years, her birthday meant gifts, cake, ice cream, parties on occasion—and something much more.

That first birthday, when my wife brought out a one layer cake with a candle flickering on a field of beige frosting, our daughter's eyes widened in amazement. She had no idea what was happening, or the difference between a carrot cake and a carrot, but this unprecedented sensation— dancing candlelight, people singing, and the aura of a special moment— drew her in and triggered a billion neurons.

The flame she could not touch invited her into a dimension just beyond her awareness, an ecstatic state like the pale line of sunrise, a consciousness she had no words to express—of her unprecedented existence, her importance to those around her, and the quality of her life.

She had only one tooth in her mouth but the small bites she took of that organic, homemade carrot cake must have had a magical effect. They stimulated her appetite for festivity. That first birthday cleared a space in her imagination for the joyous and the sacred. However, it was the second birthday that established the mythic and emotional template on which all her future birthdays would be based.

Her playgroup had only started to convene months before. Her social circle now extended beyond her parents to include other children.

At around 10 in the morning, just before I left for work, her friends started to arrive with their mothers, bearing gifts in colorful boxes. Later there would be cake and ice cream but first they played with Duplo and listened to music. Our daughter's bright, round face beamed. She babbled without speaking and moved among her friends with great excitement, popping up and down as she pointed out a feature of a toy she wished to play with. She wore a green velvet dress with a white cotton bodice and a green hair band across her golden hair.

I left early during her first party, elated by the boisterous noises of excited children. Our daughter's happiness, her luminous eyes, porcelain doll face and the barely articulate chirrups of approval and instruction she directed at her toddler guests, gave me the courage and logic I needed to drive the icy roads to my four classes in light and darkness.

When I returned to our small apartment at ten o'clock that night, after driving a hundred miles of dark, snowy superhighways and clearing a hill of ice for parking, our daughter was still beaming on the throne of her mother's lap. All day, a procession of neighbors had dropped in to wish her a happy birthday. It was the only time Alice, the previous super's eccentric daughter, ever visited our apartment. She gave our child her vintage doll with a large, ceramic face and a red silk dress. Our daughter's arms were draped around its neck.

Our daughter's 12-hour birthday party, mainly improvised, was an early peak experience. Though only vaguely remembered later on, it apparently conjured a numinous image and emotion, dominating her mind like a mountain beyond a veil of clouds. The event was ecstatic and dreamlike, to be interpreted and strived for but never reconstructed or reclaimed.

She internalized the message of that birthday, yet what it referenced was no longer present. It was less a vision than a wish. It echoed a sound that could be made just once since the instrument that played it, her preverbal consciousness, was replaced by words and consciousness.

Only a ritual of words and gestures might venerate and simulate the enchantment of this ephemeral melody, but she could never feel it again in the same way. We would make brave attempts with many devices—parties, gifts, meals, events and reminders throughout the day—but the miraculous cheer of that second birthday could not be replicated.

Even so, we tried. For years, we took inordinate pains to make her birthday festive, even when we had no money for a big party. On her third birthday, I played a clown in short baggy pants, a floppy wig and galoshes and spoke in a high pitched voice, to her delight even if I frightened some of her guests. On her fourth birthday, lacking the space that many of her friends' parents had to throw a large party, we drove 100 miles to spend the day with her grandparents, who made the celebration special because of their happiness to be part of it. On subsequent birthdays our daughter went to the theater or hosted sleepover parties with her friends; once or twice, I even made French toast for their breakfast. Once when I was unemployed, I spent all I had to throw her a party with a children's show at a café bistro, but I could only afford to invite half the class—a half-measure for which I still feel remorse.

As our daughter grew up, we expected her birthday to become as obsolete as old dolls, Disney videos and other "kid stuff" that teenagers jettison when they spurn childhood and dependency. But our daughter continued to treasure her old videos—and her birthday. She did not wish to distance herself from childhood but to commemorate and enshrine it.

Even when she went to college, physical separation and independence neither dampened her ardent feelings about her birthday nor our desire to fulfill the expectations it engendered.

Each year her birthday was another internal pilgrimage in which she transported herself on a feeling more transcendent than memory to a holy place in time from which those of us corrupted by bad and middling childhoods are barred. There, all she loved and believed to be good was stored. It was imperative to her to simulate the boundless sensation still inscribed in her mind, but only faintly recalled, of being attended to and entertained—the elation of early childhood when love surrounded her and *being there* was all she had to do to receive it. She never wished to relinquish that sensation.

As her parents, we were co-conspirators in these simulated flights to a toddler's delight. We took pride in our daughter's lambent nostalgia for birthdays past. Indeed, her happy childhood was one of our most successful productions, and we did our utmost to revive it, even when the emotion it tried to resuscitate grew more elusive.

Our daughter's birthday kept our family together through her inevitable departure and separation. When she attended college, we drove each year to her campus on the date or the weekend closest to it. After she graduated and moved across the continent, she flew home for the week around her birthday.

We called it a "national holiday" and observed the event with excitement and reverence, not just because we wished to please her, but because, like most holidays, her birthday commemorated a significant event in our lives and reinforced our collective identity.

My wife and I were a couple well before our daughter was born but her arrival made us a family. Hence, her birthday was not only about her— it was also about *us*; it celebrated her birth and the birth of our family. For my wife and me, her day evoked intense memories of that extraordinary and pivotal time—from trying to conceive to conception to pregnancy to birth—when our lives irrevocably changed.

When our adult daughter left home for good, we were gratified that she let us continue to play her indulgent parents. Yet an ironic awkwardness encroached upon our annual events. They seemed more like placeholders than celebrations as she became autonomous. While we struggled to redefine our relationship, her birthdays became markers of an uneasy maturity, rather than vestiges of a contented youth. Our closeness, past and present, was no longer as apparent as her widening distance from childhood. Each birthday suggested not what she had before but what she was missing now. Regardless of how hard we tried and how glad we were to be together, the birthday vision we attempted to revive faded.

Since we no longer had the human resources that made younger birthdays successful—no sleepovers, large classes, or groups of friends to take to dinner—we planned special outings for her birthdays and spent them like adult friends, visiting places where she'd never been and seeing new attractions. But these events felt more like family outings than birthday celebrations.

On one cold, misty birthday, we visited the Statue of Liberty and Ellis Island. It was a gloomy, evocative atmosphere for a birthday. The moisture in the air hung like a veil between our eyes and the iconic sites in the harbor. For her own reasons, our daughter seemed dejected throughout the day, though she didn't say why. I later learned from my wife that she was having misgivings about her career and considered giving up. She probably bottled these emotions, not wishing to ruin her birthday—for us.

The next year, on a warm late winter day, we drove up to Woodstock, New York. As we explored the town in the unseasonable sunshine, a pall of sadness hung over us. Tacitly we knew that what we were clinging to was barely there. A vital piece of our daughter's birthday was missing. We kept the date alive but no longer lived it.

This loss of connection became a crisis the next year when we put too much pressure on the event. Our daughter could not get a week off from her job, so we broke the pattern of her coming home and flew to California on the eve of her birthday. After she picked us up at the airport in the late afternoon, we went at a breakneck pace to take care of "business"—to purchase a cake and the gift we promised. The next morning we set out for Joshua Tree National Park to experience the winter desert.

That part of the birthday observance went well. We did desert things—climbed boulders and walked among the cacti against a cold wind in the pale light. But being in a car all day made me tired and petulant. Though I was seated in the back, our daughter noted my lack of exuberance. She rebuked me for not having the right attitude. "Are you forgetting what day it is?" she asked. She was right that I was not in festive mood, but I knew what day it was—I just wondered why it mattered so much.

This was heresy but I couldn't stop myself from thinking it. Yes, I was tired, but exhaustion was only the pretext. Sleep deprivation is an instrument to discover truth, not the truth, itself. It is a torture tactic precisely because it induces protected thoughts and feelings to emerge unchecked. As I sat in the backseat, subversive emotions surfaced. I asked myself why birthdays were always so much trouble. Why did we have to work so hard, watch what we said and pretend to be cheerful? It was only a birthday and I never made such a fuss about mine.

The tension of the day accumulated to the point that we later argued over the meaning of a billboard on our way to dinner. Hunger might have been partly to blame for this and a delicious dinner put us in good spirits. As we returned to our Airbnb apartment for the gifts and cake, it seemed that this might still be another happy birthday.

It was nearly midnight. The day had been strained and frangible but we pulled through. Our daughter had just opened her presents and cut three pieces of cake—the climax of the holiday—when all of the years of dutifully observing her birthday exploded with a small, mindless gesture.

I ran my forefinger along the side of the knife with which she had cut the cake and tasted a dollop of icing. It was an abstracted gaffe but in our daughter's eyes I desecrated the ritual of the cake, which required that she taste it first. As soon as my fingertip touched my lip, she cried out that I ruined her birthday. I pleaded with her that we had gone to considerable trouble to make the day a happy one. I explained that I was tired and made a careless slip, and that it meant nothing.

"How could you do this when you know how important my birthday is to me?" she cried.

"Please, just lighten up," I implored her. "It's a birthday."

"Lighten up about my birthday! Do you know nothing about me?" she demanded. "This is the most important day for me. It always has been. And you made it that way. Now *you* want to say it's not special and that I should forget about it?"

The more I tried to minimize my *faux pas*, the more she made of it and the worse she felt. She asked me tearfully why I would want to ruin her birthday. I told her I wasn't trying to do that at all, that she was blowing what I had done out of proportion, that she had no idea what it was like to have one's birthday truly ruined. I recounted that when I was a child, my birthday did not always get celebrated, and that throughout my teens and twenties I did not remember celebrating it at all.

She countered that just because I had terrible birthdays didn't mean I should give her one.

Unable to mollify her, I became frustrated and stubborn. I tried to appeal to her reason. I told her that birthdays were good, but after a certain point in life, one should be more flexible about them. This argument only increased her misery. She claimed that for me to suggest that she could ever be more flexible or casual about her birthday showed that I didn't know her at all.

To save what was left of her special day that was now asunder, I apologized and reminded her that most of the day had gone well and she should focus on that. I hoped she would let go of her agitation and acknowledge how much I loved her even if I ate a bit of icing prematurely.

She did not believe my apologies. She incriminated and interrogated me with red tear-soaked eyes, trying to reassemble with reproach what seemed irreparably broken. I tried one last time to produce consolatory understanding out of the emotional wreckage.

"Maybe what I'm trying to say is that you may be old enough now not to need your birthday to be perfect. I don't want to destroy it for you. I'm human and I made a mistake. That's what people do. One day your birthday may not be as special as it is or was. People in your life may not understand all that it means to you—and you'll be disappointed."

"That day will never happen. I won't let it happen," she cried.

Somehow we got through that night. The crying and castigation abated. We ate cake and spoke in emollient tones about how delicious it was. We praised the restaurant, talked effusively about her gift, and recalled the beauty of the desert. At 3AM, I walked with her to her car. She seemed to feel better, so I reiterated that I was sorry for my mindless slip but hoped it would not eclipse all of the good things we had done. Yet I knew my entreaty was in vain—this birthday would surely go down in infamy. We came to no mutual understanding because she had no conflict about the significance of her birthday. All of the conflict was on my side.

How could I make her understand that her experience of childhood, growing up—and birthdays—differed so radically from my own—and that I had purposely made it so? Just as she could not escape the warm, glowing ambience of toddler bliss embedded in her mind, I could not redecorate the empty space in my early childhood. Birthdays would never mean much to me because they were never special. I had no warm candlelight and caravanserai of friends and neighbors to give me joy. I did without the good feelings, managed the bad ones and developed a callus of disappointment. Was I right to prepare our daughter for the ugly facts from which I had protected her and subvert the primal birthday impressions that still sustained her? Yet, if her birthday meant so much to her, why was she miserable now, despite our best efforts?

The next year, she told us she had second thoughts about spending her birthday with us because I had ruined her previous one. I promised that I would be on better behavior this time. And since she was spending her birthday at our place there would be no jet lag to impair my judgment.

My wife and I discussed what we could do to make this birthday good enough to compensate for the previous one. Since going anywhere in cold weather meant being stuck in a car for a long time, which never boded well for family harmony, my wife suggested that we do a winter activity closer to home, like snow tubing. She located a spot nearby and had another idea—we would give our daughter a ski lesson.

I had my misgivings. I worried that she would twist a knee or break a leg, or that she would find herself in a beginner's class full of children and feel humiliated. My wife dismissed these fears. In the end, I had to agree that if nothing else, having my daughter get on skis for the first time would make this birthday memorable and unique.

So we followed the plan. The morning started well. I made French toast with Challah bread, which I had promised, and we started out early enough to give us time for any mistakes along the way.

When we arrived at the ski resort, we needed every bit of advance time to rent the equipment and obtain the necessary tickets. The class was 90 minutes long. After the instructor lectured for a while, the students started moving on their skis. When it was my daughter's turn she went several yards without falling. She looked steady and undaunted. With each "run" she went farther and faster.

My wife and I watched her from the bottom of the hill. Our feet were cold, but we were engrossed and happy. The 90 minutes went by with surprising speed. I could not believe that I wasn't bored or irritated watching our daughter ski repeatedly down a gentle slope. On the contrary, when the class was over, she asked if she could take another run. "Take as many as you like," I said.

Our daughter's introduction to skiing was more pleasurable than any family outing had been in years. She was enjoying herself and it was a pleasure to watch her learn a new skill. Education is more of a spectacle than it is believed to be. Yet our joy had a deeper foundation.

For years we had kept alive her special day. Each of us tried to make it festive, but we didn't feel the occasion as much as pay homage to it. By the same token, our daughter came home every year to celebrate her birthday, hoping to tap a powerful and elusive emotion from her childhood. This ski lesson did that for her—and for us, as well.

It was a new sensation and an old, familiar one. Watching her zigzagging 150 feet, I traveled a far longer distance with my cold feet planted in the cold slush.

Parents stood nearby, cheering on their young and teenage children. They had brought them here to nurture their talent and they took pride in their performances. As we watched and applauded our young adult daughter doing something for the first time, we were once again like these parents raising their schoolchildren.

The skiing lesson transported me to a time I never thought I'd revisit. For one afternoon, we revived a custom that had united us as a family like nothing else—enrichment weekends on the run, swimming classes, acting classes, art classes, shopping for clothing. For the first time in memory, we slipped into our old roles, helping our daughter discover what the world offered so she could choose what she wished to take from it. This was what we had been missing for years. It felt good to be parents again.

Her birthday was special once more.

My wife, my daughter and I had rolled back 15 years to renew our oldest bond and carry it forward. A parent-child relationship has no expiration date. People are children their entire lives, and parents are parents as long as they choose to be, if their children let them.

When our daughter was young, we were warned that as children get older the gift-wrapping means less than the gift inside. This is true for parents, as well.

The crux of parenthood for me would always be the hour after she was born. I stood outside the nursery, watching her wail away in a bassinette under warm lamps. The sight of her tiny figure, so isolated and distressed, made me cry, while the one other person at the window, an older woman, glanced at me in disdain. At that moment, I promised our daughter that I would always be there for her and protect her.

I fully meant to keep that vow but as she grew up, being there for her became ambiguous—more like a 24-hour hotline than a parent-child relationship. She no longer needed to be taken care of and there was less we could do for her.

We stayed close and chatted frequently. She shared her life with us, including her problems and dilemmas. We listened attentively and tried to be helpful, but her life and work had diverged from ours and we understood that our advice might be irrelevant. She knew more about what she was doing and what she was up against than we did.

Yet for one overcast Saturday afternoon, we gave her something she was too adult and practical to give herself, enrichment for its own sake.

A child learns to be free. A parent gives a child the tools to be free and then lets go. But if a parent and child are close, it's hard to let go.

At the airport homeland security checkpoint, which was nearly vacant, we stood by the ropes, paralyzed by sadness at another awkward departure. Our daughter said she didn't want to leave. We hugged her and said we didn't want her to leave. But we all knew she had to leave.

We reminded her that she had made a good life for herself in California, with a growing circle of friends and a burgeoning career, and we were proud of her for all that she had done on her own. Even so, we hugged each other and wouldn't let go. There's a part of us that never can.

MY ARMOIRE IS MY MEMOIR

In the vain attempt to hold onto life, I cling to material things as surrogates, perhaps in the hope they will fortify me against the nakedness from which I came and to which I will return.

This practice may guard me from the erosion of memory. It is also comforting to give permanence to temporary objects by keeping them close, and by caring for things well beyond their use and relevance. This is how I show respect for what human industry has made possible. It makes me feel more worthy of the Earth's bounty.

Yet as years pass in this manner of slow, careful accretion, I share space with much that I've gathered over time. These items are mine, yet they loiter in corners and by walls like shy, bemused strangers sporting nametags, who have traveled here great distances to attend several simultaneous reunions, for which I am the unifying theme and capstone event.

Some objects in this personal archive came to me from impulsive purchases; others are neglected witnesses of long-simmering desires. All signify choices I've made. They are loglines to episodes of my life. Yet when I scan the room from left to right, in a panorama of my space, all I see are stacks and shelves cluttered with items that are as remote to me as stars I may have seen in a clear nighttime sky months or years before.

It aches to think how far away I am now from the experiences that brought these old books, magazines, garments and furnishings into my life. I am struck by a terrible need to sort through them, to say my last "Good-byes" and deliver them to a bin, a new assignment, a place in someone else's life, where they can have renewed significance, as opposed to lingering in my life as ancient monuments that mock me.

In moments of restlessness and pique, I urge myself to get rid of the old clothes in my closet. After all, I never wear them though most are in fine condition. Yet a strong compunction prevents me from sporting these superannuated garments. I tell myself it's because I lack an appropriate occasion, but I know this is a convenient excuse.

A taboo seems to be in play, barring me from physically and symbolically entering the past. If I wear an old garment it will be tantamount to touching the person I was, rather than only remembering him. In so doing, I will be transgressing an ancient law—not by violating the dead, *per se*, but the person I was who is no longer living.

This must be the underlying, unstated motive, the spiritual fillip, for donating old apparel to consignment shops and charities. It's not all about altruism and a tax break, but keeping the past at a safe distance. Otherwise it occupies the space too close to home between the sacred and the mundane, a wardrobe and a memorial, where sentient beings cannot dwell at ease.

Practically speaking, these old clothes, which I have no reason or occasion to wear, take up so much room in the closet that I cannot remove one item from the rack without bringing down several others next to it.

I resolve to unclutter my closet, but before I can devise a plan, a subtle, subversive power intercedes. The weight of my history, the judge of all I have lived, felt and done, issues an injunction against removing so much as a solitary thread. A cooling off period is enjoined when arguments pro and con can be more fully considered. I have come to a crisis and must stop.

If I dispose of these clothes, I will never recollect having or wearing them. What they felt like, and the associations that cling to them, like the millions of microbes that cling to my epidermis, will also disappear. My mind will be stripped and alone in the present tense. When I stare in a mirror I will see an individual who has been here a long time but whose origins and activities are undocumented. I will lack what antiques experts call "provenance."

In the present I am a living being, but only a fragment of my full self. The expanse of my life is not to be found on my person except in the lines on my face and the knowledge in my eyes. I perceive who I am at this moment, but to access my life in its amplitude, I need to look around me.

Only as I am extended by memory into the past and through hope and aspiration into the future do I appear as I truly am.

The clothes crowding my armoire, though made of diverse textiles, are as hard and individual as grooved metal keys. They free the memories that stir inside me, sensed but unseen, pounding on the soundproof walls of my brain, as I stare in a mirror. They are not me, *per se*, but they are the record of me as a living being and the world in which I've dwelled.

There is more than one way to tell your story. Writing is the medium that comes most readily to mind but anything in your life can be a symbol—a word, a sign or an image—or a code that reveals the essence and narrative of your life.

By the same token, you can turn any aspect of your life into a text. It's probably nothing to be proud of, but my reluctance to let go of old clothes has turned my closet into my sartorial autobiography, a photo album in cloth, and each of the garments hanging there is a chapter, a paragraph or a sentence that reminds me of who I was and where I was at different moments of my life.

My armoire is arranged from right to left, with the latest garments on the left and the oldest garments at the right against the wall. It is a reverse timeline, to be read from present to past. If my life is a long sentence, I want it to begin with where I am now as the subject. If readers scan right, and are inclined to ramble, they may learn where I've been, the long predicate of how I came to be.

There, for instance, is the battleship gray sweater I once purchased after teaching classes on a Friday afternoon. The sales associate who helped me, a dark haired woman in a tangerine blazer and a purple skirt, said, "I'd never look twice at someone in that gray sweater."

"Really?" I asked, chastened. "I'll take it anyway."

She shrugged. I told her that I never intended to wear this gray sweater to a club, but only to stand in front of a group of students, as if this excused my gray soul and anodyne taste.

"I see your point," the vividly clad woman replied. "Still, they may fall asleep when they look at this sweater."

"They may fall asleep anyway," I conceded.

To study my history in this way puts it in realistic terms. A gray sweater purchased more than 20 years ago is not so much a sentimental memento as a piece of information on a missing person—the man I used to be. How can I be sentimental about a gray sweater?

Yet when I stare at this remarkable garment, intact but for one perfectly round moth hole over the heart, and hold its coarse fibers in my hands, it becomes a pass-card to a vault of rare, forgotten footage that memory now projects through the darkness of my mind to illuminate my present. I watch such vignettes, which the sweater restores and reenacts in vivid detail, with pleasure and gratitude.

In items as mundane as the clothes I chose I note values and virtues I wished to cultivate. For instance, I selected a coarse gray wool sweater when I was teaching because I strove to portray myself as a serious man doing a professional job.

It is good that I can review my life in this way, not as an epic that features me as a hero, but as someone who led not necessarily the most interesting life, but an authentic one with its tales of pain and laughter.

One fine attribute of being alive you can rely upon is that you don't need to be the same person from beginning to end. It may not even be possible. Age and experience change you, despite your wishes and intentions. Life's new tenant differs from the longtime resident who faces eviction. Circumstances help form who I am and who I will become. I may wish to believe otherwise—that I am the same through all vicissitudes— and it is true that parts of me remain constant if I am lucky: I think with the roughly same mind and perceive with the same senses. Yet the objects I ponder and perceive have changed and have different meanings.

Who we are is not just inside of us, under our skin and in our heads. A penumbra of words and deeds, activities and encounters, envelops us. Clothes and accessories are the shells and husks we've left behind in our tumultuous strivings now reduced to a low hum. These soft casings seem like silent and indifferent witnesses, yet they bear traces of us and testify to our styles, sizes and self-images changing over time. If we have the patience and curiosity to review this stationary parade, our closets and their contents can tell us a good deal about this external, contextual, aspect of ourselves—albeit not always in the most direct manner.

This is why my closet is an expert chronicler of my development.

Some may ask why I need to recapitulate what I've already lived. Our living, breathing lives move in one direction—toward the future. Yet memories of a life lived are also part of the present and future. They are alive, though dormant. The past sleeps and awakens only when we think of it, but we are always moving in it as it moves through us.

In a restless moment, I admonish myself to purge the clutter. There is no room in my mind and living space for artifacts of isolated moments that left no trail or legacy. I know where to start.

As I stand transfixed before this tiny storeroom of relics and refugees from my past, which I will never wear again, I run my fingers along sleeves and seams, attempting to devise a process of elimination. Still, I can't decide what is irrelevant and worth tossing. This frustrates me. I know I must free myself from useless things and clear space for the future, yet a strong, subversive undertow prevents me from extracting garments from the rack. I scrutinize the clothes, seeking reasons to eliminate this shirt or that pair of pants to no avail. If I evaluated them strictly on their quality and appeal, it would be simple to clear half the closet, but their appearance is irrelevant to their retention.

These shirts, ties, jackets and pants test my memory, but I can exercise my brain in other ways. No, it is fear that prevents me from removing a shirt with a frayed, yellow collar, a faded T-shirt with a split seam, and pants I cannot button. I am afraid of losing my life, not just the one I lead now, but the one that came before. The moment I occupy is exiguous and thin and I barely feel it passing, but the clothes crushed together in my closet fill and restore the years that can still be counted and accounted for.

These garments offer winking hints. They challenge me to talk about them and around them, the circumstances in which I purchased them, and the eras when I wore them. Their labels and designs tell me what I was thinking, doing, and hoping for when I saw them on a rack or shelf and tried them on. They remind me what they meant to me and how I felt about the world and myself when I wore them. They testify to what I lived and how I lived at a time I only dimly remember and to parts of me that otherwise would go missing. These useless clothes are relics, and empty as shells, but I fear that if I throw them in a box and get rid of them, I will become a shell.

I extract from the rack a green linen shirt without pockets that I bought one summer, and I study it. How beautiful it was and how impractical! Where would I slip in a pen or a tissue for my allergic rhinitis? There are the three blue and white summer shirts—one with checks, another with stripes and a third with a tiny hounds-tooth pattern. I bought them at J Crew just after I started a job that went well before it ended a year later in acrimony.

These shirts remind me of warm mornings crossing Rockefeller Center between its skyscrapers, mosaics and bas-reliefs. They recount soft, golden evenings and long walks across midtown, up Broadway, to the subway at Columbus Circle. It is amazing how easily one invents patterns of living. Such habits make the world seem new, then become embedded in the mind long after they become as archaic as the shirts on the right end of my armoire. I was middle-aged when I wore these shirts, yet the world seemed new when I wore them. This must be the principal reason for buying new clothes and for keeping them. They reassure me that life can renew itself as fresh and vital, and that I can respond to it in kind.

As my fingers smooth over shirts toward the center of the rack, I come to a dividing line where buttons and collars give way to crew necks. This is more than random or capricious. It marks a watershed in my personal history, when my professional status changed from staffer to freelancer. This shift in style indicates a sea change in my self-perception. I had been a full-time employee trying without success to play a corporate game emphasizing teamwork and process at the expense of personal fulfillment. I tried to fool others and myself into believing I was the man who wore the collared, buttoned shirts, ties and blazers. I could never be that person but I could look the part and I prided myself in my performance.

When I went freelance, I shifted to simple T-shirts, and compensated for this lack of sartorial variety by having these plain shirts in an array of colors. During my first winter as a freelancer, I worked with a young art director who dressed up his habitual T-shirts under soft sweaters. I admired this simple, elegant style, which bespoke comfort and taste, and emulated it. I stocked my wardrobe with cashmere sweaters and have rarely worn a buttoned shirt for years unless I attended a wedding, a funeral or a job interview.

This closet is deep and has a second rack, reserved for old sports coats, suits and ancient pants. There I can find a green velvet novelty jacket, short sleeved and embroidered with sparkles and musical notes. This sartorial oddity goes way back to my rock and roll days and it might make a fine if incongruous match for the black leather pants that hang near it, but both are too small to try on, even for laughs. Near them hang a pair of vinyl pants which I acquired at a store called "Trash and Vaudeville" on St. Mark's Place. I made this purchase due to economy—I couldn't afford leather. When I wore these plastic pants, held up by striped suspenders, no less—someone in the audience at the Botany Club where I performed, shouted, "Nice plastic pants!" I didn't give that fan an autograph.

One of the more elegant and humorous articles of clothing in my armoire of memories is a trimly tailored plush corduroy brown jacket with large square pockets. I found it at Peterman's, a store once located at the Grand Central Terminal facing East 42nd Street. I learned about this store from an architect who designed the store's interiors—he was the father of a child in my daughter's kindergarten class. Since I worked nearby, I went into the boutique and found there an unusual assortment of clothes and accessories, attractively displayed.

What made Peterman's a unique and famous retailer was its

catalogue. The Peterman's Catalogue, of which I still have some samples, was written like a literary anthology. Each item had a vignette of a paragraph or two that seemed to be ripped out of a character's journal, letter or memoir. It was all inventive and beautifully written but also a clever marketing concept since it gave these mass-produced items an "aura" of one-of-a-kind specificity.

I ended up buying the plush brown corduroy blazer, as well as two heavy oversized cotton sweaters that sit on the closet's shelf with boxes of old manuscripts. The one jacket on the store rack had been a size too small, so the manager made a few calls and located the same jacket in the right size and had it shipped to my home.

Of course, such a wonderful store could not survive in a world of mass-marketed schlock where there is no sales help, and the clothes seem to be manufactured in the same mindless factory. I later learned that Peterman's was a running joke on *Seinfeld*. Of course, why not take a cheap shot at the only retailer who produced literate ads? Ironically, the Peterman's style of selling with stories was far ahead of its times. With all of the free space on the Internet that craves content, a narrative style of retail marketing could make a comeback on websites and online retail.

The most universal time marker in a closet is the size of a garment. I know women who dedicate a section of their closet to the pants, skirts, dresses and outfits they once fit into when they were their "perfect size." These aspirational garments remain as mementos of what their owners were and wish to recapture. As time drags them off against their will to maturity and old age, these garments remain immutable artifacts of a dream they may have attained but that they can never regain. Perhaps they never need to, since the small sizes testify to the admiration they inspired.

I have my own ghetto of obsolete jeans to the extreme left of the rack pressed against the wall. They do not represent an ideal size. Rather, they are now so large on me that my belt on the tightest notch cannot prevent them from slipping down my legs. I wonder as I look at these jeans how they ever fit and how I could have believed they looked good on me. I must never have seen my true size and how much smaller I was than the clothes

I selected.

This delusion of girth, if not of grandeur, was deeply ingrained in me. When I was a boy I bought oversized clothes, no doubt because subconsciously I wanted to be bigger than I was. These oversized pants in my closet are evidence of the largest version of me, but when I lost weight, true to my old self, I continued to buy the larger size. These roomy pants remain in good condition and seem to belong to a different man. It required a lifetime for me to be aware of my body size and to find clothes that fit properly. My closet provides a timeline not only for how my body evolved, but my perception of it.

History seems long to us, but it is a brief segment on an infinite line. Personal history is no different. The record of what I know about myself is a fraction of all that I've forgotten, never known, and may never know. Similarly, the clothes in the armoire, though crammed together, are only a percentage of the clothes I've lost, worn out and thrown away.

One also may come to a time beyond history, when artifacts of the past cease to be relevant because one has lost the impetus to revisit them. I wonder if I need to return to the days symbolized by the checkered shirt with the shiny collar, the skinny polyester tie, the threadbare tweed jacket, the pleated khakis or the flannel suit. From the moment we no longer wear an old garment, is it truly of use to us? Whatever it says about our old selves may no longer be relevant. By suggesting this, I know that I may be casting in doubt the premise of this essay as well as my rationale for keeping old clothes. This argument has yet to be settled in my mind.

A clothes closet isn't the only medium that may connect you with the life you've lived, but one resource among many. You may prefer a photo album, but in my home this calls for a field trip and a detour. I must interrupt my life to seek the massive tome in its hiding place, extract it from its dusty storage and squat on a floor as I turn its plastic pages. By contrast, the clothes closet is integral to my life, and only moonlights as an archive of the past. It contains not just the man in the mirror, but the life traveler. Until a proper time machine is invented, my closet will suffice.

FINAL THOUGHTS

When I first contemplated writing this book my intention was to replicate the tone and purpose of the self-help genre for satirical ends. But the danger of parody is that it can become sincere.

This has been especially true with the theme of self-help because of two stubborn facts: we all need help, and it is as hard to obtain from others as love and money. Our only recourse is to help ourselves.

Self-help ought to be simple but it isn't. Before we can help ourselves, we have to know ourselves, which our outward-facing culture distracts us from doing. Knowing oneself is hard work, so we would rather do what we can to avoid it.

Finally, when our evasions end in a cul-de-sac, we're led to believe we're unequipped to help ourselves and require professionals to rescue us.

All of this convinced me that a serious need existed for practical advice, after all, and the spoof became real.

Apparently, regardless of how many others are in our lives, lasting help is often nowhere to be found but in ourselves.

I wrote these essays in the spirit of camaraderie, hoping that a word or phrase would provide insight, comfort—even laughter—to readers. I believed that if kindred individuals identified themselves in the distorted real life experiences related here, they would be relieved to learn that they are not alone in trying to fathom and navigate the world. If their perceptions and responses were confirmed in these pages, they might also gain confidence.

If this book has achieved any of these outcomes, it has been worth the time and effort in writing it.

Made in the USA
Middletown, DE
15 July 2021